LET IT
FLY!

Defy the Laws of Business Gravity
And
Keep Your Company Soaring

Gary Lim, M.A.

◆
DORATO PRESS

LET IT FLY! DEFY THE LAWS OF BUSINESS GRAVITY AND KEEP YOUR COMPANY SOARING. Copyright © 2009 by Gary Lim. All rights reserved. Printed and bound in the United States of America. No part of this book may be used or reproduced in any manner whatsoever without written permission except in the case of brief quotations embodied in critical articles and reviews. For information address Dorato Press, P. O. Box 71, Manlius, NY 13104.

FIRST EDITION

Publisher's Cataloging-In-Publication Data

Lim, Gary.
    Let it fly! : defy the laws of business gravity and keep your company soaring / Gary Lim. -- 1st ed.

    p. ; cm.

    ISBN: 978-0-615-20865-7

    1. Leadership--United States. 2. Employee empowerment--United States. 3. Management--United States. 4. Success in business--United States. I. Title.

HD57.7 .L48 2009
658.4/092   2008905212

For further information:

315-885-1532

www.LetItFlyBook.com

Dedicated to my wife Judy, who not only flies with me,
but who also travels with me on the Road to Gumption,
and to our daughter, who kept asking me
if I was done writing *Let It Fly!* yet.

Also by Gary Lim

The Road to Gumption:
Using Your Inner Courage To Balance
Your Work and Personal Life

Introduction

The so-called "war for talent" has been waged on corporate fronts for years. As cycles of the economy ebb and flow, the need to attract and retain talented associates and managers takes on even more importance.

Central to this objective is the premise that some of the best people will be attracted to company environments that allow them to excel at what they do. Someone who is good at what she does typically wants to focus on getting the job done. This person is innovative, responsible, and accountable. She's not very likely to want to hear that she should be doing things the way someone else wants them to be done. Nor is she likely to enjoy spending an inordinate amount of time repeatedly summarizing progress or explaining what's next.

I believe most of us are intuitively aware that to "let it fly", that is, to let our people excel, is the right thing to do. For those associates who we identify as exceptional, we rarely need reminding. But what about the rest of the pack? There are very good people in this group, too. And if we don't give them a chance to "let it fly" in their own right, we might lose them in the war for talent.

In the parable **Let It Fly!** , the two fictional characters explore these issues in the non-fictional setting of the Pebble Beach Golf Links at scenic Pebble Beach, California. Meet Carl Baxter and Ed Hilland. One is the epitome of letting it fly, while the other is of more traditional management philosophies. During their round of golf, Carl shares with Ed the virtues of letting it fly, along with some tips for implementation.

The core theme is an iterative leadership cycle called **FORE™**. This is an acronym signifying four phases: Focus, Offload, Review, Encourage. In each of the phases, we discover the notion of the **Laws of Business Gravity™**. These are five "laws" that if ignored, will drag a company's growth to the ground, perhaps even taking the company down as well.

In each phase of FORE, we are made aware of a corresponding Law of Business Gravity that we must try to "defy" to keep our company soaring. The tips to remember are called **Aerial Views**™ and serve to remind us to execute the FORE cycle and to try to defy the Laws of Business Gravity.

FORE, Aerial Views, and the Laws of Business Gravity. Like the golf metaphor that is woven into this story, the analogy is there. In golf, defy Newton's laws of gravity (with high-tech golf balls and clubs), and you keep your golf shot soaring. In business, defy the Laws of Business Gravity (with FORE and Aerial Views), and you keep your company soaring.

I wrote this book with the intent that the lessons be useful at any level of leadership, whether you lead a large or small company, for-profit or not-for-profit, a division, a department, a group, a team, or other entity. Simply replace the word "Company" in "Keep Your Company Soaring" with your entity.

Whether you are a golfer or not, may you hit it long, high, and down the middle. Now let it fly!

Gary Lim
info@LetItFlyBook.com

(Note ... for storytelling purposes I took some literary license with the setting. Carl and Ed play an entire round at Pebble Beach Golf Links as a twosome, with no other golfers in sight, either in front of or behind them. You would not likely encounter the same conditions.)

Contents

Prologue – Two Golfers

The early morning sun shone brilliantly on the white building, glinting off the roof's shingles and peaks, highlighting the white columns on the walls. Over the double doors was a simple yet elegant sign, gold letters on a black background, "The Lodge." Another beautiful morning at Pebble Beach Golf Links, with its timeless Lodge overlooking the storied 18th green where, since the early 1920's, so many famous golfers have holed out the last putts of their rounds. Walk through the front double doors, head toward the back porch, and catch the view that just takes your breath away – the spectacularly crystal blue waters of the Pacific Ocean, the sweeping coastline, and the mountains rising in the distance beyond.

In the parking lot across the street from The Lodge, a rental car pulled abruptly into an open spot, the squeal of its tires piercing the morning quiet. Ed Hilland threw open the driver's door and launched his body out of the seat, landing on his feet with a dull thud. A man of average height with a definitively round build, Ed's silver-white hair reflected in the sunlight as he walked back to the trunk and lifted the lid.

Despite the fact that he had for a long time been looking forward to playing the Pebble Beach course, Ed was not in a particularly good mood. He had already spoken to his East Coast office, where the corporate-owned manufacturing company he had been president of for the past 10 years was located. Whenever he traveled, Ed usually called in at least a couple of times a day, with his first call today at 5 o'clock in the morning, California time. That made it 8 o'clock Eastern time, and Ed was irritated that the receptionist wasn't there to answer the call. It didn't matter that hers was a planned absence, and that someone else answered the call just as promptly.

Ed liked calling at 8 o'clock sharp, just to see who was in the office on time and who wasn't. He was of the old school, where you were supposed to be at your desk, ready to work, at the appointed hour.

Touching base by phone with all members of his company's management team, he wanted to hear what each manager was going to accomplish during the day. If Ed didn't like something he heard, he told them so, issuing instructions on how certain things should be done. By the time he hung up the phone about 90 minutes later, he was on a slow burn, shaking his head at the things that always seemed to drop through the cracks whenever he was away.

In the last two or three years, profitability had become more and more difficult to achieve, as the marketplace for the company's products shifted with the changing economy. Growth had been there in the early years, but lately had leveled off. Financially, it felt like they were only treading water. For these reasons, Ed felt he needed to personally monitor most of the operations. He was just frustrated that if he was away from the office for even a short time, it appeared that some things didn't get done.

During the past few months Ed had not been able to sleep well at night, worrying about the business. Though he didn't like to admit it even to himself, he was not sure what to do next. The company's growth had been flat in recent years, and he wasn't sure where future growth would be coming from. There were rumors that the corporate parent might be seeking to sell the company, and those rumors just made Ed that much more nervous about his job security. The hourly employees didn't care to go the extra mile, asking about overtime for any minute worked beyond regular hours.

Ed was finding himself in a dilemma that appeared only to get deeper. With the company's lack of growth, even as president he felt like he had little control over his destiny. Company issues and problems were determining his actions. He could stay the course and continue to fight fires, but he couldn't figure out how to get around the lack of motivation on the part of his employees. On some days he thought he was the only one in the building who cared. Maybe even on most days.

Trying to get away for a few days' vacation time, Ed and his wife traveled to the San Francisco Bay Area since she had never visited. The round of golf at Pebble Beach was a gift from his wife, and also a convenient excuse for her to go shopping in nearby Carmel.

Ed muttered to himself as he started to unload his golf bag from the trunk of the car, thinking about the morning's earlier phone conversations. "Can't those guys ever get things right. I have to set them straight each and every time." He shook his head again and started to change into his golf shoes. When he was finished, he slung his golf bag over his shoulder, locked the car and stomped off in the direction of the pro shop to sign in for his round.

M oments later, a few spaces down from where Ed had parked, another rental car drove into an open spot and came smoothly to a stop. Carl Baxter got out of the car and strode to the trunk. Tall, athletic build, with dark hair, he had the air of calm, understated confidence about him. Lifting the lid, he started to unload his golf gear.

He too, was on vacation, from the distribution company he owned in the Midwest. Starting with just himself and a partner 12 years before, he built the business steadily, adding the right kind of people when it was the right time to do so. After a few years, the firm grew to a level of revenue and headcount where he could afford to take at least 3 weeks off each year, sometimes more. Today Carl's wife chose to remain in San Jose to visit with some of her relatives while Carl lived his dream, playing at Pebble Beach Golf Links for the very first time.

Whenever Carl went away on vacation, his personal rule was to never call his office. He didn't even really look at his BlackBerry all that much either. If it became necessary, his managers could call Carl's cell phone, but they knew that would have to be an extreme case. In the last 5 or 6 years, Carl had never been called. He wouldn't want to receive a call anyway, because something pretty serious would have had to happen for his management team to call him while he was on vacation.

As Carl sat on the rear bumper of his rental car putting on his golf shoes, he paused for a moment and took in the early morning sight of The Lodge with its pristine white walls, the bright green of the surrounding grass, and the brilliant blue of the ocean beyond. "Boy, what a view," he said softly to himself, pursing his lips in a silent whistle.

Carl stood up, locked the car, picked up his golf bag, and headed toward the practice putting green to stretch and warm up.

Chapter 1 – FORE!

The starter in the Pebble Beach pro shop looked over the list of tee time reservations for the morning. It wasn't a terribly busy morning, but there would be a steady stream of golfers, though well spaced. That would allow the golfers to play at a comfortable pace and enjoy themselves. He looked up as a tall man, dressed for golf, approached the counter and spoke.

"Good morning … I'm Carl Baxter, and I have an 8:03 tee time, I think."

The starter looked down at his schedule sheet and said, "Yes Mr. Baxter, I have you right here. You'll be playing with Mr. Hilland today."

"Okay," said Carl, as he fished for his credit card in his wallet. "Hopefully I won't be holding Mr. Hilland back too much!"

"No sir," said the starter with a smile, reaching out to take Carl's credit card. After taking care of the payment, the starter handed Carl's card back to him. "Thank you, Mr. Baxter. We may actually be running a little ahead this morning, but you still have a few minutes before you need to head to the first tee."

"Sounds good, thanks very much," replied Carl. He strode out the door to retrieve his golf bag. Since he had already stretched and taken a few putts, he decided to head to the first tee and scout it out. Carl slung the bag over his shoulder and walked toward the waiting area.

The air was cool, the sun was bright – it was indeed a perfect morning at Pebble Beach.

He arrived just in time to hear the announcement over the public address system, "Next up, Mr. Baxter and Mr. Hilland." Carl felt a surge of adrenaline, hearing his name echoing at Pebble Beach. If only it were "Next up, Mr. Baxter, Mr. Woods, and Mr. Mickelson." Another golfer who had already been waiting approached him.

"Good morning, you must be Mr. Baxter," said the golfer with a smile, extending his hand. "I'm Ed Hilland."

"Carl Baxter, nice to meet you." Carl shook Ed's hand and smiled back. "I have to confess, this is my first time playing here, so maybe you could show some mercy on me." He laughed.

"Well, it's my first time, too," admitted Ed. "So it's more a matter of whether the course is going to show any mercy on both of us!" His smile turned to a slight scowl. "Besides, my morning already got off to a lousy start, so it can only get better from here, right?"

Carl didn't know what to say in response, so he just busied himself with his golf bag, pulling out sleeves of golf balls and fishing for tees. After getting situated, he looked over and asked, "So, are you a guest here at Pebble Beach, Ed?"

Ed chuckled, "I wish, but no. We're staying in Monterey, and this round of golf was a gift from my wife. I've always wanted to play here. What about you?"

"Always wanted to play here, too," replied Carl, playing one-handed catch with a golf ball. "I just haven't had the opportunity to do so until this trip. We're staying up in the San Jose area where my wife has some relatives. I got up early to make the drive down here." Carl put the ball in his pocket and started to gently swing a 3-wood he plucked from his bag.

"What's your line of business?" asked Ed, pulling out a driver.

Still swinging the club, Carl answered, "I own a distribution company in the Midwest. We're a full-line distributor of supplies and equipment for the plumbing industry. How about you, Ed?"

With his driver held horizontally behind his neck, Ed was doing some gentle twisting. "I'm president of a manufacturing company back East, owned by a large private corporate parent. We make home furnishings and accessories, mostly ready-to-assemble."

The public address system came to life again. "On the tee, Mr. Hilland and Mr. Baxter. Enjoy your round, gentlemen."

The men walked up to the tee box. Carl said, "Ed, go ahead and hit if you're ready. Believe it or not, I'm actually a little nervous. It's like I've been waiting my whole life for this moment. And there's not even much of an audience!" He looked around and laughed.

Ed grinned. "Lucky for me nobody's watching." He teed up his ball and stepped back to look down the fairway. "So, dogleg right, huh?"

"Yep," replied Carl, "but you want to stay left because it won't do you any good to try to cut the dogleg. I think I'm going to aim in the direction of that first fairway bunker on the left."

Ed turned to look at Carl, his eyebrows arched. "I thought you said you never played here before!"

Carl grinned and pointed to his head. "That doesn't mean that I haven't played here in my mind, over and over again."

Ed took a practice swing then stepped up to address his ball. He hit a low ball that went in the direction of the bunker that Carl mentioned, but well short. Picking up his tee, he looked at Carl, shrugged, and said, "Oh well, off the tee safely anyway."

Carl moved into the tee box, teed his ball up, and stepped back to look down the fairway and get his line. He took a practice swing, addressed the ball, and took a deep breath. Taking a nice easy swing, Carl launched the ball into the air. His ball landed in the left side of the fairway and rolled along the line he was aiming for. Just the shot he was visualizing all those years.

Ed looked at where Carl's ball had come to rest, and then looked back at Carl. "Looks like it's you who should show some mercy on me, Carl." Ed laughed, a sort of derisive-sounding laugh.

Carl grinned sheepishly at the implied compliment. "Thanks, I'm just happy to get my first tee shot at Pebble Beach in the air."

The golfers gathered their golf bags and started walking down the fairway, falling in step with each other.

"What type of home furnishings do you guys make?" asked Carl.

"Oh, different things you might use in your home," answered Ed, carefully stepping over a sprinkler head. "End tables, folding chairs, computer desks, bookshelves … that sort of thing. Pretty much all ready-to-assemble, or 'RTA' as we say in our business."

They both came to a stop near Ed's ball. Ed surveyed the scene, selected a club, and lined up his shot. He swung, but the resulting mishit sent the ball into the rough on the right side of the fairway, about 75 yards from the green. Ed swore softly to himself, but it was loud enough for Carl to hear.

Ed dumped his club back into his bag, and both men started to walk toward Carl's ball. "What about you, Carl? What are your products?"

Striding forward, Carl answered, "We're a distributor for the plumbing industry, so we sell to small independents and some franchise networks. Just about anything you can think of, fixtures, components, supplies, and assemblies."

They reached Carl's ball laying in the fairway, where he had a straight shot to the green. Carl selected a club, went through his pre-shot routine, and let the ball fly. It arced gracefully, perfectly visible against the blue California sky, and landed right in the middle of the green.

"Nice shot," said Ed grudgingly.

"Thanks," Carl said, as he put his club back in his bag. He looked up to see Ed walking off toward his ball in the right rough.

Taking some quick steps to catch up, Carl asked, "So how's the economy affecting your business these days?"

Eyes focused on his ball as he approached it, Ed answered, "It's been challenging, but I think for me it's less the economy and more the type of employees I have."

Carl looked at him as they stopped near Ed's ball. "What do you mean, 'type of employees'?"

Ed replied, a slight edge creeping into his voice, "You know, it's like the old saying, you can't get good help anymore. Lately I've been feeling like I have to clean up after my employees all the time."

He looked down at his ball, up at the hole, and selected a club. Waggling it a bit, he looked at Carl and asked, "Do you have a tough time finding good people where you are in the Midwest?"

Carl waited until Ed hit his ball. It lofted into the air and landed just short of the green, on the fringe.

"Nice shot," said Carl. "I don't know that I have a 'tough time' finding good people where I am, but I do have to move out one or two people once in awhile if they don't work out."

"Well I do that too," agreed Ed. "We lay off folks when we're not as busy."

"No, I didn't mean that," corrected Carl. The two men had taken their putters from their bags and were walking onto the putting surface. "I meant that if a member of our team doesn't work out, we have to move that person out. But it doesn't happen very often."

Ed stopped and looked at Carl. "So you don't do layoffs?"

"No."

"I take it you haven't been growing much, then," said Ed as he started to examine his ball's path to the hole.

Carl felt a momentary flash of irritation at Ed's assumption. "Actually, we've grown anywhere from 30 to 40 percent each year over the past 5 years," he replied in a deliberately pleasant tone. "Your shot – go ahead and knock it in the hole, Ed."

Ed stood over his ball and swung the putter a couple of times before putting from the fringe. The ball skipped a little before settling well short of the hole. He shook his head.

"Well, I guess I'm still away, aren't I?" he asked. Carl nodded silently. Another putt by Ed brought his ball close to the hole, and he tapped it in. Bending over to pick it out of the hole, Ed said, "Well, it's good to get the first one under my belt."

Carl, who had already lined up his putt earlier, stepped up to his ball. As he started his routine, Ed said,

"So how did you manage that kind of growth with the swings of the economy?"

In the middle of his practice stroke, Carl stopped and looked up at Ed. "I'll share the secret with you in a moment, if you'll let me take my best shot. It's not every day that I get a chance to putt for birdie, and at Pebble Beach yet."

Carl concentrated again on his ball, and stroked his putt. The ball stopped just short of the hole, and he tapped it in.

"Not a bad start!" exclaimed Ed, as they walked to where they had left their golf bags. "Now what's the secret for growing your business?"

Carl slipped his putter back into his bag, and leaned on the tops of his wood covers for a moment. "I think you said earlier that you had to clean up after your employees all the time. I give direction on where we're headed, but let my teammates figure out what they need to do for us to get there."

The two men started walking to the 2nd hole. Ed asked, "What do you mean, 'teammates'? You mean your management team?"

Carl looked at him and answered, "My management team, their team members … as far as I'm concerned, everyone in my company is my teammate."

Ed grinned and said sarcastically, "C'mon, you can't tell me that a guy in your warehouse is your teammate. Your role is a whole lot more important than his is."

"Absolutely he's my teammate," replied Carl, being deliberately patient with his tone as he returned Ed's gaze. "And there are many times when his role is way more important than mine, because I'm not the one who is getting the shipment out the door." He walked ahead to the tee box and started to look down the fairway.

Ed pulled a driver from his bag. "Well, my employees are not enough of team players to be called teammates. Most of them are just there to collect paychecks, and I'm the poor soul signing them." He swung his club a couple of times.

Carl thought for a moment about what Ed had just said. "Out of curiosity, Ed, what's your growth been like over the past few years, and how big is your company? That is, if you don't mind telling me. We're not competing in the same industry, and at the moment we're alone in the woods here." Carl smiled and gestured around him.

Ed stroked his chin as he pondered his answer. "To be honest, we've been pretty flat the last couple of years or more. That's why I've had to really stay on top of my guys, to make sure they're doing the right things. My company is running about 45 million dollars in revenues, with anywhere from 140 to 180 people, depending on how busy we are." He leaned on the end of his club. "What about yours, Carl?"

Carl swung his driver gently as he stood at the edge of the tee box. "We should do over 40 million dollars this year, and I have about 70 teammates." He bent over to tee up his ball, then looked at the hole information. "Let's see, par 5, 502 yards. You have to fly about 200 yards to clear the first bunker."

Ed pursed his lips and whistled, still thinking about Carl's revenue. "Not bad – but I'll bet with all that revenue and so few employees, you're busy when you travel, keeping tabs on things." He laughed.

Now in his pre-swing routine, Carl looked down the fairway before answering. "Actually, when I'm on vacation like I am now, my rule is to never call the office." He swung and launched the ball on its way. It came to rest at the very beginning of the short grass, another shot that he had been imagining all these years.

Ed stepped up to the tee and looked after Carl's shot. "Nice shot. My turn to lay it out there." When Ed hit his ball, it flew straight, but landed short of Carl's.

As they walked toward the fairway with their bags over their shoulders, Ed turned to Carl again. "How can you be away and not call in? I have to call at least twice a day," he complained.

Carl returned the look. "It's beginning to occur to me that you have a fairly hands-on approach to managing your business, is that right?"

"Yeah, what's wrong with that? After all, I'm in charge!" Ed sounded defensive.

"Nothing – it's just an observation, not a criticism." Carl kept walking, looking straight ahead as he continued talking. "In my case, I've found that delegating to my teammates leaves me with a lot less to worry about. That's why I don't need to call in. I know my teammates will handle things. Besides, if they really needed my help on something, they would call me."

They slowed as they reached Ed's ball. "But that would have to be an extreme case," finished Carl.

Ed selected a club from his bag. "Well, I think you're darn lucky to have people you can count on. I wish I were lucky enough to find people in my area like that," whined Ed. He took a practice swing.

"You might want to be careful of that deep bunker that's about 75 yards in front of the green," cautioned Carl. To the sight of Ed's raised eyebrows, Carl grinned. "Remember, I've played this course in my mind a hundred times."

Ed hit his ball and watched it fly. The ball sliced to the right and landed in the rough. He muttered a choice phrase under his breath that didn't go unnoticed by Carl.

Carl picked up from Ed's previous comment. "I definitely am lucky to have the people that I have, but I doubt that my area is the only area where you can find them," he remarked dryly. Choosing to avoid the bunker, Carl hit his second shot to about 100 yards from the green, in the middle of the fairway. The two men started walking again.

"I really don't know how you do it. I can't leave my guys alone without checking on them, and when I do, I always find something screwed up." Ed was almost stomping his way down the fairway at the thought of his interaction with his team earlier this morning.

Carl looked over with some amusement. "So you wouldn't consider letting them do their jobs, with a little less hands-on from you?"

"Nope, couldn't do that. That's too much risk for me. I want to make sure things come out right." Ed looked down at the grass as he walked and talked. "It's my neck on the line, if something gets screwed up. These days, I'm a little nervous about my job security."

Carl was silent for a moment, deciding whether to say what he had in mind. He stopped in mid-stride and gestured for emphasis.

"The way it was for me, I had to learn to let go," Carl started to explain. "It's like golf, at some point you have to 'let it fly' and not lay up. In my business, I was eventually able to let go – let it fly – and let my team excel. And when I did, that's when our growth really started to kick in." The two men started to walk again.

"Well, you're a better gambler than I," admitted Ed as they neared his ball in the rough. "Maybe if I had better employees, I could do that." He peered at the ball, sitting deep in the grass. Looking up at the hole, he selected an iron.

Carl waited silently while Ed lined up his shot. On its way, the ball cleared the deep bunker that ran the width of the fairway, but landed in the small bunker just beyond.

"Dammit, I hit that one fat," seethed Ed.

Carl walked over to his ball, sitting in the middle of the fairway. Taking out his wedge, he started to line up his shot as Ed approached.

"Just out of curiosity," asked Ed, "how do you decide when to let go and when to pull on the reins?"

Taking a practice swing with his club, Carl stood behind his ball and looked beyond at the flagstick on the green. Without answering, he stepped up to the ball, and launched it in the air. The ball arced high and dropped onto the middle of the green, rolling away from the flag just a bit. As Carl lowered his club from his follow-through, he turned to Ed.

"It's really not a matter of deciding when to let go and when not to." Carl slipped his club back in his bag, and took out his putter. The men started walking toward the green again. "It's a matter of letting go and letting your team do what they do best."

"But I don't have many situations where I can trust my guys," Ed protested. "It just seems like they're always looking to me to tell them what to do." He stopped as they reached the bunker where his ball had landed. Grabbing his sand wedge in one hand, Ed picked up the rake in the other and walked onto the sand. It took two tries before the ball came out and landed at the edge of the putting surface. Ed muttered another epithet under his breath and tossed his wedge in the direction of his bag.

As Ed raked the sand, leaving what seemed to be an even bigger hole, Carl remarked, "Well maybe they're coming to you all the time because they think you want them to. Do you want them to?"

Ed emerged from the trap, picked up his golf bag, and fell in step with Carl. The two dropped their bags off to the far side of the green, in line with the next tee. Ed pulled out his putter and answered the question. "No, of course I don't. They ought to know what to do, but sometimes they drive me crazy asking should we do this, or should we do that." Holding the putter in one hand, Ed swiped at the fringe next to the green, irked at the thought.

Carl rested his putter on the ground and leaned on the handle as if it were a walking stick. "That's what I mean – maybe they think you want them to check with you. You told me earlier that you have to call in twice a day, so doesn't that seem to suggest that you want to hear the details?"

Irritation flashed across Ed's face. "Well of course I have to call in!" he almost shouted as he gestured angrily. "If I didn't, things would probably never get done right!"

With that outburst, Carl pretended to survey the green where their golf balls lay. "Well, let's see, I guess you're away, Ed," he said. Carl started to walk over to where his ball sat on the putting surface, leaving Ed bending over to line up his putt.

The next few moments passed in silence, with both men concentrating on making their putts. The tricky green extracted three putts from each golfer. As Carl holed his ball out, Ed said, "Not a bad start, Carl, one over after two holes at Pebble Beach." He clapped Carl on the shoulder.

"Thanks," said Carl with a smile, by now wondering what kind of round he was in for with his playing partner. They collected their bags again and headed for the 3rd tee, just a few steps away.

"What I was saying earlier," Carl began carefully, "was if your people *think* you want them to check with you, they will, even if that's not really what you want. Maybe you need to make your wishes a little clearer."

Ed, standing by the ball washer, looked over at Carl and replied, "That's why I was asking you earlier about letting go. I can't tell in advance which are the situations where I can turn them loose, and which aren't."

Carl teed up his ball, stepped back, and loosely swung the driver in his hands. Gazing down the fairway, he said, "You don't look at each situation individually, you follow a process that sets the tone for how you work with your team." He turned and looked at Ed. "I call it my FORE system … F-O-R-E," explained Carl, spelling out the acronym for Ed.

"And what does FORE stand for?" asked Ed, a bemused grin on his face. "But never mind that now, go ahead and tee off." He waved his hand in the direction of the fairway.

"Okay, I'm going to try to skirt those trees on the left," said Carl, "and if I'm lucky, get a little draw out of this." He took a breath, and sent the ball on its way. "Aw, shucks, pushed it," he said, as the ball stayed straight and landed in the right rough, barely missing the first of a string of bunkers alongside the fairway. He picked up his tee and shrugged.

"That'll work. At least you stayed out of the sand," remarked Ed as he stepped into the tee box. A moment later, Ed's drive landed at the very beginning of the fairway, in the short grass. "All right, my first fairway hit!" he yelled, arms above his head, celebrating. Carl grinned.

They started walking again. Ed turned to Carl and said, "So what does FORE stand for?"

"Simple," replied Carl. "Focus, Offload, Review, Encourage. It's the way I remind myself to let go – let it fly – and let my teammates do their thing. I use a golf metaphor so it's easier for me to remember." He chuckled.

"Sounds pretty logical," agreed Ed. He hitched up his pants. "But it doesn't sound all that revolutionary, if you know what I mean."

"Maybe not," said Carl, "but for me anyway, it's been the key to our growth over the past few years. And I'm almost certain that if I hadn't followed this line of thinking, I might still be stuck working too many hours with not much to show for it."

Ed shot a look at him to see if he was implying anything with that last remark, but Carl was looking out at the ocean as it came into sight from behind the trees. He stopped in his tracks. "Man, can you believe that view!" gushed Carl as he looked down the length of the fairway at the flagstick on the third green. Beyond, the bright, deep blue of the Pacific Ocean met the paler blue of the sky at the horizon, highlighted by a few wispy clouds above.

"Well, it's great that you've got the right kind of people so you can apply your FORE system," said Ed with a touch of defensiveness.

"Actually, it's FORE that allowed me to see what types of teammates I really wanted to work with," explained Carl enthusiastically. They were now standing at the fairway's edge, between both golf balls. As Carl started to get swept up in his explanation, he momentarily forgot about his next shot.

"And I use FORE with another golf metaphor," he continued. "You know how the newest golf balls are designed to try to defy the laws of gravity as long as possible, to keep the ball aloft?"

Ed nodded. "Yeah, it has to do with the number and shape of dimples, right?"

"Well, I've got what I call the Laws of Business Gravity." Carl was really starting to warm to the topic. "Just as the laws of gravity pull a golf ball down to the ground, over time the Laws of Business Gravity pull a business down to the ground. And if you don't defy these Laws, you're history." He suddenly remembered that they needed to play their next shots. "Oh, sorry, go ahead and hit." He grinned and gestured at Ed, then started to walk to where his ball lay in the rough.

Ed called out to Carl's retreating back, "Okay, but when we get to the green, I want to hear about those Laws of Business Gravity!" Carl gave a thumbs-up sign without turning.

Recap – FORE!

In Chapter 1 we were introduced to the metaphor of the FORE™ system, which includes 4 phases:

F = Focus
O = Offload
R = Review
E = Encourage

With each phase there are associated Laws of Business Gravity™. As Newton's law of gravity works to pull objects (like a golf ball in flight) down to the ground, the Laws of Business Gravity™ work to pull a company's growth down. You must try to defy the Laws of Business Gravity to keep your company growing and soaring.

A central theme in being able to defy the Laws of Business Gravity is to be successful at assembling a team of people who you can trust and rely on. The FORE™ system is based on leading your team of associates in a manner that allows them to excel at what they do best. When you allow them to "let it fly", that is, trust them to do their best at what they do, they have the freedom to excel. That lets you focus on the things you really need to focus on as a leader, like creating growth opportunities.

Get ready to learn more about FORE, and the tips that go with each phase to help you defy the Laws of Business Gravity!

Chapter 2 – "F" is for "Focus"

The two golfers advanced toward the green of the third hole. Ed was able to hit his second shot fairly straight, landing in the fairway at the entry to the green, between the two bunkers. Carl's ball was also laying nearby, but it had taken him two strokes to get to that point, the thick rough gobbling up most of his first try. Ed walked down the middle of the fairway while Carl took the route through the longer grass on the right. The men approached their golf balls and each other again.

"Took me an extra shot to get back in the short stuff," Carl complained mildly.

Ed shrugged. "Bad break. But at least you're clear to the green." He gestured straight ahead.

"Maybe so, but this green is hard to read, so I'm not exactly home yet," said Carl as he squinted to survey the putting surface.

"So, back there you started to mention your Laws of Business Gravity," reminded Ed, picking up where they left off at the beginning of the fairway. He reached into his golf bag and picked out a wedge. Taking a couple of practice swings, he waited for Carl to respond.

Carl straightened and turned to Ed. "That's right. Like the laws of gravity taking a golf ball back down to the ground, the Laws of Business Gravity will hold a company back and eventually take it down. You need to defy these Laws if you want to grow your business and keep your company soaring like a good golf shot." He pulled out a pitching wedge from his bag. Swinging the club gently in one hand, Carl continued his explanation.

"Here's the first Law:"

> ## FIRST LAW OF BUSINESS GRAVITY.
>
> **'WITHOUT A LONG RANGE PLAN, A COMPANY'S GROWTH WILL EVENTUALLY DECREASE UNTIL IT BECOMES NEGATIVE.'**

"So you defy this Law by making sure you have a long range plan that your teammates buy into as well." Carl turned back to look at the green and start scoping out his next shot.

Turning to the green as well, Ed remarked, "Well, isn't that pretty obvious? I mean, the need for a long range plan?"

Carl had just finished a practice swing. Resting the club shaft on his shoulder, he turned. "Maybe, but you'd be surprised how many companies, particularly small or even midsize businesses, haven't written one." With a sideways glance at Ed as he turned back to his ball, Carl asked, "Do you have one?"

Ed bristled at the implication. "Why of course I do! What business leader doesn't have a plan?" He stared at Carl, who was getting ready to hit.

Carl swung and lofted his ball high in the air. It landed on the green and rolled away from the hole, coming to a stop about 25 feet away.

"I'll take it," said Carl with a shrug, turning back to Ed with a smile. "I didn't mean that I didn't think you had a plan, I was just asking if you had written one, and also if you've shared it with your teammates."

Ed started to take a bead on his shot. As he looked the green over, he replied, "Well, we have some things in writing, but it's pretty clear in my mind where we need to go. As for sharing it with my employees…" He laughed, somewhat scornfully, as he focused on his golf ball. "Like I said, 'long range' for a lot of them is something like the upcoming weekend. I don't think they'd really care that much about a long-range plan." Ed swung, sending his ball into the air. It landed and rolled to a stop about 30 feet from the hole, opposite the flagstick from where Carl's ball was.

Carl watched Ed's ball come to a stop. "Well, what works for me is to put it on paper and get my team to understand the picture. Major parts of the plan are created by my senior associates anyhow. No, I don't necessarily give every single teammate a copy of the plan, but I make sure they understand where we're trying to go." He carried his bag to the side of the green closer to the next hole, and took out his putter.

With putter also in hand, Ed walked onto the green. "Well, like I said before, lucky for you, you've got better people to choose from in your neck of the woods." His smirk matched the sarcastic tone of his voice.

Carl was in mid-step when he stopped and turned. Looking first at the ground then directly at Ed, Carl's eyes flashed an angry and penetrating stare as he quietly said, "Look Ed, I'll make you a deal. You stop implying that it's just dumb luck that I have great employees, and I'll be happy to share some of my experiences with you. That is, if you're interested. 'Cause if you're not, just say so, and we can find other things to talk about. This topic just happens to be one I'm very passionate about." Carl abruptly turned away and walked over to his ball.

Ed shifted his weight uncomfortably, feeling the awkwardness of the moment. "Uh, I apologize," he called out to Carl. "I didn't mean it that way. And yes, I'd like to hear about what you've done. Your firm is almost the same size as mine in revenues, but you only have half the headcount. It probably would do me some good to learn more."

Ed squatted down to view his putting line. "I have to admit, I feel like I need to make changes, but I don't really know what I need to do," he added quietly. "And that's not something I'd readily confess to anybody." He stood up again. "Sometimes I feel like I'm being yanked by my chain."

"By the way, I think you're away," said Carl, allowing Ed the first putt. "Deal – I'll tell you about my growth system, with the caveat that you can take the advice in the spirit of the money you paid for it." Carl laughed heartily, dissipating the tension.

The cagey third green caused Ed to take three putts to hole out, while Carl was able to put away his ball in two. They marked their cards and started to walk to the 4th tee, crossing the path between the 16th and 17th holes. Carl stopped short and looked to his right, at the sight of the Pacific Ocean beyond the flagstick waving gently on the 17th green. He could see whitecaps near the horizon amidst the blue glassiness of the water.

"Can you believe it?" He was almost beside himself. "What a view – I've been waiting twenty-five years for this!"

Ed laughed at Carl's exuberance. "Okay, young man, calm down."

The two men continued to the 4th hole.

Ed looked down the fairway from the tee area and observed, "Par 4, 327 yards, huh? Should be no problem." He snorted and looked over at Carl, who was pulling a fairway wood from his bag.

"There's a fairway bunker running crosswise that you want to carry," warned Carl. "I think it's about 170 yards out. And, of course, water on the right!" He laughed, gesturing at Stillwater Cove. The sun glinted off the surface of the water in the distance, rippling to the beat of the currents.

Grinning, Ed said, "Go ahead and hit when ready." As Carl fished for his golf ball from his pocket, Ed asked, "So, your system for creating growth in your company is the FORE concept that you mentioned earlier?"

Carl was trying to find his tee. "That's part of it. Basically there are three things to keep in mind." He found his tee and bent over to tee up his ball in the ground.

Straightening again, he continued, pausing in the middle of his setup routine. "There's **FORE**, which as I said stands for Focus, Offload, Review, Encourage. Then there are **Five Laws of Business Gravity**, which I remind myself to defy, so my company doesn't get dragged down to the ground. And finally, there are a set of rules to keep in mind that I call **Aerial Views**. These are 7 tips I've developed to remind myself to 'let it fly', to keep my company soaring."

Carl grinned and asked, "Make sense?" He turned back to address his ball.

Ed waited until Carl hit his ball and watched it fly. The ball cleared the bunker and landed in the middle of the fairway.

"Sounds like a lot to remember," replied Ed as he started to tee his ball up. "FORE, Aerial Views, Laws of Business Gravity. Nice shot, by the way."

"It really falls into place when you put it into the perspective of FORE," said Carl enthusiastically, almost forgetting about his great golf shot. "Look at FORE as a series of recurring steps or phases. Each step of FORE – that is, Focus, Offload, Review, Encourage – has one or two Aerial Views associated with it. And the Five Laws of Business Gravity are really just reminders for you to keep your eye on the ball, so to speak. So I view my job as company owner and CEO to make sure I keep the process going – Focus, Offload, Review, Encourage."

Ed stepped up to his ball and launched it. The ball started straight, then sliced to the right, heading to the ocean. It dropped into the rough along the right side, between the bunker and where the grass dropped away to the waterfront.

"Now if I could just apply your Laws to straighten out my golf shot!" he said to Carl.

"Can't help you there," replied Carl, as they started down the fairway, bags slung on their shoulders. "But let's talk about the first step, F in FORE, for Focus. There is one Aerial View that goes with this phase, and it is … well here, let me give you the card." He stopped, rummaged through his golf bag for his wallet, then took out a small card and handed it to Ed.

Ed squinted, trying to read the small print. "I'm going to need my reading glasses for this one," he complained.

"No problem," said Carl, "we'll just talk about what's on the card, and it's yours to keep to remind yourself later. So, for the Focus phase, the first Aerial View is …"

Aerial View #1.

When you wish upon a star, make sure everyone knows what the star looks like.

Ed listened and nodded. "That's what you meant by sharing your plan with your employees."

"Right." They had reached Ed's ball in the right rough. Momentarily oblivious to the gorgeous view of the Pacific coastline just yards away, Carl continued.

"Your teammates have to know what the star looks like, or else they won't be focused. And you'll have to remind them periodically of what that star looks like – how big it is, how it's shaped, how far away it is, everything about it that they can visualize." Carl was gesturing skyward as he spoke.

Taking a club from his bag, Ed walked over to stand behind his ball and line up his next shot. As he looked toward the green, he asked, "But what level of detail are we talking about? Give me an example of what a star might look like."

"Enough detail so your guys can visualize it," replied Carl, fiddling with a tee in his pocket, "but not so much where they get bogged down. Besides, if you give too much detail, then not only do they lose focus, but you end up micromanaging."

He paused for a moment while Ed took his stance and let his ball fly. The heavy rough grabbed the clubface, and the ball landed well short of the green but in the fairway. Ed watched the ball roll to a stop, then looked down, shaking his head.

Carl continued, "By the way, as you'll see when we get to talking about the rest of the FORE cycle, you can't leave out any letters."

"Leave out any letters?" Eyebrows raised, Ed was swinging his club idly with one hand.

"Think about it. If you do only Focus, Review, Encourage, and leave out Offload, then you're stuck doing everything yourself. If you do only Focus, Offload, Encourage, and not the Review part, your teammates might be headed in the wrong direction if something unexpected happens. And if you do Focus, Offload, Review, but no Encourage, then you could soon have a dispirited team because they don't get any kudos."

Ed thought about this. "And I suppose, if I did the Offload, Review, Encourage, but not Focus, they wouldn't know where we're supposed to be headed?"

"Right. They might not know what the star looks like or where to find it."

The two men walked a few steps over to where Carl's ball lay in the middle of the fairway. Carl picked up where he left off. "So, back on your question of what the star looks like … maybe it's your revenue goals, or your gross margin targets, or the number of new accounts. Things that your people can quickly understand and relate to."

As Carl eyed his next shot, Ed leaned against his bag and countered, "Well, some of those things I consider confidential, and don't care to share with my employees."

With a look of surprise, Carl turned to Ed. "You mean no one knows what your financial objectives are for your company?"

A bit defensively, Ed replied, "Well, of course my direct reports know the numbers, my controller, operations manager, and sales manager, but they're not supposed to share it with the rank-and-file. Those guys might think they're entitled to more money."

"Then … how do they know how they're doing?" asked Carl carefully. He turned back to eyeing his ball, and selected a club from his bag. After a practice swing, he hit his shot. Carl's ball arced through the air, landed on the green in front of the hole, and rolled back a few feet in the direction of the fairway. Both men started to walk toward Ed's ball.

Answering Carl's question, Ed said matter-of-factly, "They know how they're doing by the kind of job they're doing. Whether they're doing good work, on time, and with a minimum of screw-ups."

Carl glanced at Ed and even more carefully asked, "Who determines the difference between 'good work' and a 'screw-up'?"

It was Ed's turn to look at Carl in surprise. "Why, I do, of course," he replied. "Don't you?"

"Actually, no," said Carl. "My teammates come up with the standards of how to measure their performance."

Ed looked at Carl in disbelief. "Are you kidding me? You let them tell you whether they think they're doing a good job or not? Doesn't that let them shoot for a low target?"

The men reached Ed's ball sitting in the fairway grass. As Ed reached for a wedge, Carl answered. "Remember from Aerial View #1, I've already defined the star I'm wishing on. I let the teams figure out how to get us to the star."

Ed stood behind his ball to line up his shot, stepped up to take his stance, and let the ball fly. It landed on the green and rolled to a stop about 30 feet from the hole. He returned his club to his bag, hoisted it to his shoulder, and started walking again.

"I'm not sure my guys could figure that out," said Ed shaking his head. "They always come running to me asking all sorts of questions as it is."

Carl looked straight ahead as they approached greenside. Eyes narrowed as he squinted at his ball, he said, "Well, you do need the right people on the team in order to take this approach, but I'll talk more about that later. Right now, I think you're away!" Both men again left their golf bags on the far side of the green, near the tee box for the 5th hole.

The golfers each went over to their golf balls laying on the green. Ed started to line up his putt. He went first, pushing his ball wide of the hole. It took two more putts for his ball to drop, causing Ed to mutter some more choice phrases under his breath.

"Another double," he said with a big sigh.

Carl had been carefully looking his shot over. This was another opportunity for a birdie, not a short putt, but at least straight uphill. He stood up, assumed his stance, and putted. The ball went straight at the hole, then caught the right edge and lipped out as both men groaned simultaneously. Carl went over and tapped in for the par.

"Nice try anyhow," said Ed, as they walked off the green to their bags.

Carl looked up from marking his scorecard. "And I thought I had it!" Both golfers, bags in hand, walked over to the tee box of the 5th hole.

Ed frowned as he thought about what Carl had said moments earlier. "You mentioned that you need the right people to take your FORE approach. I don't want to get in trouble with you again over this, but if I just can't find the right people in my area, how am I going to make that work?"

Carl put his golf ball in the washer and pumped the handle. "Let me ask you this first. What kind of people do you feel you have now?"

"I told you, they're short-sighted guys who appear to be focused on what advantage they can get on the company. And they seem to need me to tell them what to do most times." Ed, taking his turn at the ball washer, was working the handle vigorously as he talked.

"Do you think that sharing your objectives – the Focus phase of FORE – would cause them to act differently?" Carl looked out to his right, over the gentle ripples of Stillwater Cove.

"I don't see how it would," Ed replied, following his gaze.

Carl turned and locked eyes with Ed. "Why do you say that?"

Ed stared back, then looked out on the Cove again, frowning. "I ... just don't think they'd be interested in hearing it. I think they're more focused on wanting to know what to do to earn their pay."

"That's almost like saying your associates don't care to be anything more than drones." Carl was being careful with his sentences. "Is that really what you're saying?"

"Well, I told you I have a tough time finding the right people! Now let's play some golf!" barked Ed, abruptly turning back to the hole.

Carl backed off. "Okay, let's see, we've got 142 yards. I would say the safest would be to aim for the left-center of the green." He once again noticed how much it irritated Ed to talk about his people.

Recap – "F" is for "Focus"

In the FORE™ system, the first phase "F" stands for **Focus**. As the leader of your team, you solidify the vision of and direction in which your company should be headed. While it is most effective to build consensus as you formulate your long range plan, the end result needs to be clear to your organization.

You can't leave out any phases of FORE. For example, if you **Focus** but don't **Offload**, you micromanage. If you **Offload** but don't **Review**, you might go off course. If you **Offload** and **Review**, but don't **Encourage**, you'll have some burnt-out people after awhile. And if you **Offload**, **Review** and **Encourage**, but didn't **Focus** beforehand, then you run the risk of getting things done tactically but getting nowhere strategically. All four phases work together.

We were introduced to the first of the Laws of Business Gravity™:

First Law of Business Gravity.

"Without a long range plan, a company's growth will eventually decrease until it becomes negative."

To defy this Law of Business Gravity, the first Aerial View™ comes into play:

Aerial View #1. When you wish upon a star, make sure everyone knows what the star looks like.

(Recap continued on next page …)

(... continued from the previous page)

Your teammates should know how far away the star is, what it looks like, how big it is … make it vivid. Translate that into metrics that your team relates to, such as revenues, profit margins, satisfied customers, quality levels, new products per year, market share, or anything else that best fits your company's business objectives and target markets.

If everyone knows exactly what the star looks like, you collectively have a much better chance of making that wish (objective) come true.

Having a long range plan that is communicated clearly to everyone will help defy the First Law of Business Gravity. The plan doesn't have to be long, complicated, or involved. It just needs to be clear so it can be easily understood.

Chapter 3 – "O" is for "Offload"

As they stood at the tee of the 5th hole at Pebble Beach, each man was silent for a moment, envisioning their next shot. A large bunker lay in line between the tee and the flagstick, along the bluffs at the edge of Stillwater Cove.

"Can you tell where that wind is coming from right now?" asked Carl, looking to defuse the tension of their last exchange.

"No," complained Ed. "It feels like it's coming from everywhere. What are you going to do?"

Carl reached into his bag and pulled out an iron. "I think I'll put it up there and play it like it's going to blow to the left, and see what happens." He stuck a tee into the ground and put his golf ball on top of it.

Turning to Ed, he grinned and said, "I'll just let it fly!" Carl went through his routine and stepped up to hit his ball. The ball sailed high in the air, seemed to hang a bit, and drifted to the left. It landed on the left side of the green and rolled to the edge.

Walking up to the tee, Ed shook his head. "Nice shot. Came out just like you called it!"

Ed launched his ball, which flew straight at first then started to curve right. The wind held the ball up long enough for it to drop into the front sand trap.

Muttering under his breath, Ed clunked his club back into his bag.

"Well, look at the bright side, Ed. I think the wind helped you stay out of the Cove," remarked Carl mildly.

"Yeah, but look at the size of that overhang in the bunker!" exclaimed Ed as the two men walked up the fairway.

Suddenly Ed stopped walking. Carl stopped too, turning to see what happened. Ed looked straight at him.

"Okay, I'll admit it. Maybe I can be a bit of a control freak, so maybe I do want my guys to ask me for direction sometimes. But how else will I know they're on the right track?"

Carl put his bag down and leaned on it. "Let's look at the second Law. Got your card?" Ed fished it out of his pocket.

SECOND LAW OF BUSINESS GRAVITY.

'HAVING ALL THE ANSWERS IS NOT THE ANSWER TO GROWTH.'

Ed read it and the golfers started walking again. "You mean that I shouldn't have all the answers. But isn't it up to the guys like you and me to make the hard decisions?"

Carl nodded his head. "I would agree, but I think that's the case only some of the time, not often." The golfers reached the bunker where Ed's ball had landed.

Carl continued, eyeing Ed's ball in its half-buried lie. "In my case, most of the time my teammates have way more information to make a key decision than I have. In those cases, they make the decision on their own."

"Then how do you know what's going on? If it's a major decision, wouldn't you want to have any say over it?" Ed asked as he pulled his sand wedge out of his bag.

"Of course I would," answered Carl. "If it's major enough, my managers might already know what they want to do, but check with me to see if I concur. It just depends. They all know me well enough to know whether they need to check with me in advance or not."

Ed had climbed into the bunker and was setting up his stance. "I'm going to give this a whack now, look out below!" He caught it thin. His ball rocketed off the club face, hit the lip of the bunker, and bounced backwards onto the grass surrounding the trap.

"Well, at least I can hit it from there." Ed laughed as he raked the sand smooth.

After he laid the rake down, Ed picked up from Carl's last point. "Sounds pretty arbitrary, though, what you said about your guys knowing whether or not to come bother you about a decision they make."

"First of all, it never bothers me if they need to come see me," corrected Carl. He stepped backward a few paces to give Ed clearance to hit his next shot. "As for it being arbitrary … I suppose so. The knowledge comes from the amount of time we've spent working together and getting to know each other as a team."

Ed was sighting his next shot from the grass. The last thing he wanted to do was to end up in the bunker again. With his wedge he took a smooth swing, and the ball flew up and over the trap, landing and rolling across the green until it was stopped by the first cut of fringe.

"Whew, swung a little harder than I needed to, but I didn't want to end up in the same place." Ed looked at Carl, who winked.

"Nice shot."

The men carried their bags around to the left side of the green in the direction of the 6th tee, and walked onto the putting surface with their putters.

"Let's come back to the last Law of Business Gravity that you mentioned, 'Having all the answers is not the answer to growth.' " Ed pointed at himself. "If I don't have all the answers, and my guys certainly don't have the answers, then who does?"

Carl stood by the flagstick, again looking out onto Stillwater Cove as he thought about Ed's question. Turning, he said, "This comes back to having the right people on your team." He suddenly held up his hand. "I know what you're going to say!" Ed's mouth started to open as if he were about to interrupt.

"I know you're thinking you can't find the right people. But the fact of the matter is, you have to find the right people. If you don't, you don't stand a chance of growing. And if it's bad enough, you don't stand a chance of even surviving."

"In fact, Aerial View #2 addresses this. You'll see it on the card I gave you." Ed reached into his pocket and pulled out the card. Carl pointed at it.

Aerial View #2.

Find the right teammates, then find out what makes their jobs easier.

"But that's where I'm in a quandary," whined Ed. "I don't seem to have that pool to choose from."

"Okay, more on that after we putt out," said Carl, using his putter to point at Ed's ball on the fringe. "You're up first."

The golfers finished the 5th hole. Ed needed two more putts once he was on the green, and finished with a 6. Carl's birdie putt stopped about 3 feet short, but his par putt lipped out and he had to settle for a bogey. Bags on shoulders again, the men started off for the 6th tee.

Carl continued their previous train of thought. "I know you think that you don't have the right people in your area, but I really think it's an issue of not looking through the right pair of glasses."

Striding alongside, Ed looked at Carl inquisitively. "Right pair of glasses?"

"Yep. Listen, I appreciated your honesty when you admitted to feeling – on occasion – like you need to be in control. Let's take that one step further. What if you telegraph that part of you more than you think? That could influence the type of people who remain interested in working at your company."

The golfers reached the 6th hole tee box. Carl stopped, turned around and took in the view from the tee. The blue of Stillwater Cove peeked through the cypress trees on the right, and straight ahead, the deeper blue of the Pacific Ocean met the sky blue at the horizon. Cotton ball puffs of clouds floated in the distance. It was a crystal-clear morning, and Carl could almost taste the freshness of the air.

"Can you believe this?" Carl stretched his arms wide. "What a view! I'm actually on the 6th tee at Pebble Beach!" He could hardly contain himself again.

Ed laughed. "Okay, young man, get a hold of yourself. Besides, I think you have honors – again."

As Carl rummaged through his golf bag, Ed continued, "What do you mean, about the way I'm influencing the type of people working for me?"

Pulling a driver out, Carl answered, "Let's look at it this way. You feel that you're good at what you do, and that you don't need much direction to do what you do, right?"

Ed nodded in agreement.

"Suppose you interviewed for another general manager's position at another company. If the guy you're supposed to report to tells you that he wants to be informed about every single thing you do, and wants to approve every decision you make, what would be your reaction?"

Ed's response was immediate, as he stood there swinging his driver loosely. "Why, I'd say 'thanks but no thanks' and look somewhere else."

"Right, you wouldn't be interested. So if – and I'm not saying you do this – but if you convey a similar image to someone interviewing with you, wouldn't you think they would have a similar reaction, if they were at all like you?" Carl pointed at Ed for emphasis.

"But these guys don't have the same level of experience as I do," Ed replied, holding his driver shaft behind his neck in a stretch position.

Carl stuck his tee into the ground and straightened. "That's not the point. Whatever level of experience they have, they might feel that they're good at what they do. So if you act like you don't think so, and that you're going to check everything they do, they might not be interested either." Carl stood behind his tee to survey his upcoming shot.

The 6th at Pebble Beach is the second most difficult hole on the course. From the tee, it looks like the fairway drops, runs, then swoops up sharply and to the right, ending at an elevated green 500 yards away.

"Okay, let's see if I can let it fly and put the ball in the left side of the fairway landing area. What do you think?" He grinned and looked at Ed, who gave him a thumbs-up.

Carl stepped up, went through his waggle, and let it fly. The ball sailed straight and then with a slight draw, landed at the left edge of the fairway before rolling into the first cut of rough.

Holding his follow-through pose while looking downrange, Carl said, "I'll take it. At least I stayed out of the bunker."

"Nice shot," agreed Ed as he stepped up to prepare for his shot. "Sure looks like a long hole from here."

"Yeah, we still have to get up that steep hill at the end to get to the green." Carl was squinting down the fairway. "I'll bet the flag will look like it's on the top of a 10-story building by the time we approach it."

Ed went through his routine and launched his ball. This time it went straight and stayed straight, landing in the middle of the fairway. He did a mock dance. "In the short stuff!"

Carl grinned. "Nice golf shot, Ed."

"Well, I'm entitled to at least one of those every round." Ed put his driver back into his bag and slung it over his shoulder. "Back to what we were talking about. So you think I might be chasing away the independent thinkers. What am I supposed to do, find a bunch of clones of myself?"

The two men set off for their golf balls. "Actually, no," answered Carl with a sly grin. "That would violate the next one of my Laws of Business Gravity."

Ed shot him a sideways glance. "You've got one for this, too?"

"Definitely. You'll see it on your card. The third Law is …"

THIRD LAW OF BUSINESS GRAVITY.

'HIRING PEOPLE WHO ARE TOO MUCH LIKE YOU, OR WHO LIKE YOU TOO MUCH, WILL LIMIT YOUR GROWTH.'

Ed kept walking, eyes ahead. "Very interesting. Care to say more?" he said with a touch of sarcasm.

Though Carl picked up on the sentiment, he ignored it and continued. "If you have a group made up of clones of you, then you won't have the diversity of perspectives or experience. They'd all be you, and you wouldn't get outside your own box."

Bristling at the implication, Ed started to say, "Now wait a minute, I've got great …"

"I'm not saying that you're not experienced," interrupted Carl. "I was just saying that multiple occurrences of your own point of view don't offer you any new perspectives."

They came to a stop near Ed's ball. "Okay, I guess I can agree with that," said Ed grudgingly. "What about the other half of that Law, about people who like you too much?"

Carl surveyed the fairway in front of them, with the steep slope rising up and sweeping to the right, leading to the flagstick perched at the top. His eyes on the 6th hole flag fluttering in the distance, he answered Ed.

"If you hire too many people who like you too much, then you won't get very many dissenting points of view. And you won't get much bad news either. The people who like you too much won't want to disappoint you or run the risk of upsetting you.'

Carl turned and looked at Ed. "I don't know about you, but if one of my teammates feels strongly enough about something, I want to hear about it, even if I happen to have a different opinion. And I certainly want to hear any bad news as soon as it happens."

Ed took out a fairway wood from his bag. "Well, I would agree with you there also."

"So the ideal goal is to have a group of diverse, experienced team members who can explore different points of view, and who are focused on doing the right thing for the company instead of on keeping the boss happy." Carl gestured to Ed's ball. "Go ahead and hit. Put it on the green. Better yet, in the hole!"

Ed laughed. "Yeah, right. But, to use your words, I'll 'let it fly.' " He swung his club. The ball rose, staying straight, and hit the top of the approach slope, rolling out of sight from their point of view.

Letting out a whoop, Ed cried, "All right, my second shot in a row without a slice! On a roll!"

Offering up a high-five, Carl grinned. "Very nice. See what happens when you just 'let it fly'?" They started walking over to where Carl's ball lay in the first cut of rough.

As they came to a stop, Ed said, "Let's get back to that tip you mentioned before, Aerial View #2. Say I've found the right teammates. Tell me more about what you mean when you say 'find out what makes their jobs easier'."

"Just exactly that," said Carl, pulling a fairway wood out of his bag. "See what they need to get their jobs done better, faster, easier, and with a greater sense of satisfaction. On my team, I just ask." He started to swing the club loosely.

Ed thought about the response for a moment. "Don't they ask for everything? Well, not everything, but wouldn't they ask for more than you can deliver, or afford?"

Carl nodded. "It happens at times, but that doesn't stop me from asking what they need. I don't guarantee that a request will result in a fulfillment of the wish. I don't even guarantee that I'll agree with the request. But if I don't ask, I might never know."

Turning toward his target line, Carl said, "Okay, now it's my turn to hit a golf shot like yours." He lined up his sights and swung away. The ball soared high and soft, clearing the top of the hill and landing out of sight, but obviously a good golf shot.

"Nicely done," muttered Ed as he started to walk again.

Carl fell in step as they cut over to the left side, following the path uphill to the level of the green. He returned to the topic at hand.

"Remember, all this about finding the right people speaks to the phase that we're discussing right now. It's in the FORE cycle – Focus, Offload, Review,

Encourage. We're talking about the Offload part of the cycle, where you offload or delegate things to your team and let them shine."

Ed glanced at Carl as they walked along. "I'd love to do that. But again, my biggest problem is finding the right type of people for me to have the confidence to do so."

Carl looked straight ahead as they approached the top of the hill, with the full expanse of the Pacific Ocean rising into view. "I don't want you to take this the wrong way, Ed, but maybe you should think about how you're coming across to those who work for you. If everyone thinks that you want only people who will 'listen and do,' instead of 'think and act,' that's what you'll get. Regardless of what you would like to have."

Ed considered this for a moment and pursed his lips. "Well, maybe you've got a point there. I do tend to have a strong personality sometimes, and I'm sure it comes across."

Carl grinned at Ed's understated remark. "Probably more than you realize," he said. He stopped to survey the results of their golf shots. Ed's ball was in the first cut of rough, short of the fairway landing area, and his own ball was in the fairway, dead center. The view beyond the golf balls was breathtaking, straight out over Stillwater Cove, and overlooking the tee box of the 18th hole of Pebble Beach and The Lodge in the distance.

"Looks like it's your shot, Ed," called Carl.

"Okay, let's put the FORE talk on hold for a minute, while I concentrate on this hole. I might have a great hole coming!" Ed started to line up his shot and selected a club from his bag. A minute or two later the ball was on the way, a high arc lifting toward the green, landing softly and rolling to about 25 feet from the pin.

Ed let out an even louder whoop. "On the green in regulation! I can hardly believe it!" He danced his jig again, arms raised in jubilation.

Carl grinned broadly. "That's three great golf shots in a row. Let's see if some of that rubbed off on me." He started his routine and launched his ball. Carl's ball bounced onto the front edge of the green, but two hops later, it ran through and off into the fringe.

"Aw, shucks," he said, "thought I had a good one."

"Should be okay from there," commented Ed. The men dropped their bags at the side of the green and took out their putters.

The next few minutes were quiet as the golfers concentrated on their shots, particularly with the chance to make par. Carl elected to use a 6-iron to do a chip and run, but needed two putts to get the ball into the hole. Ed had already putted once, and was looking at about 4 feet for his par.

In a loud mock-whisper as he lined up his putt, Ed said, "And the crowd is hushed as Hilland looks at this difficult putt for par. Can he do it?" Carl grinned, and Ed launched his putt.

"Unbelievable!" Ed shouted, as the ball clattered into the cup. He raised his arms. "I have made par at Pebble Beach!"

With a big smile, Carl walked over and gave Ed a high five. "And on one of the toughest holes of the course! Congratulations!"

"I've even got honors on the next hole, to boot!" Ed was practically beside himself, much to Carl's amusement.

The players replaced their clubs in their bags and walked over to the tee area for the 7th hole. They stood for a moment surveying the view from the elevated tee box onto the small green below surrounded by water on three sides. It looked like the ocean's waves could lap up at any time and wash over the putting surface.

"Hmm, 106 yards," muttered Ed. "The hole looks like it's practically in the water."

"Yeah, but feel the wind swirling?" Carl held his hand up. "That's the tricky part."

Both players decided to take short irons to try to hit knockdown shots, keeping the ball out of the wind. Having honors, Ed stepped up and put his tee into the ground, then placed his ball on top.

Turning to Carl with a slight frown, he said, "So how do you know which requests to approve?"

Carl blinked, then realized that Ed had resumed the discussion of Aerial View #2, about finding out what makes your team's jobs easier. "That falls into the category of owner's prerogative, I guess. Usually I ask a bunch of questions and try to understand the impact of what's being requested. Then I go with my instinct."

Turning back to his ball, Ed nodded, and said, "Okay let's see what I can do with this." He took a short swing and launched the ball at the hole below. The ball drifted to the right and landed in the bunker on the right side of the green.

He shrugged. "Oh well, at least it's dry."

Carl stepped up and teed his ball. He went through his routine, and swung. The ball went straight and low, boring through the breezes to land on the green below.

Ed looked at where Carl's ball lay and said sarcastically, "Well, I think I know who's got honors on the next hole." The golfers gathered their bags and walked down to the green.

"I just think that if I ask my guys what they need in order to do their jobs better, they'll be asking for the world." Ed pulled his sand wedge from his bag. "And I can't afford the world."

As Carl selected his putter, Ed continued, "Besides, if you ask the question 'What do you need?', don't you get into a cause and effect discussion? If you don't give him what he wants, doesn't that make it easy for him to later say that he couldn't do his job because you didn't give him what he asked for?"

"You mean, asking them what they need would essentially give them an excuse for not doing their jobs?" asked Carl. Ed nodded.

"No, it doesn't give them any excuses." Carl was swinging his putter, holding the grip with just his thumb and forefinger. "I just ask them what they could use to make their jobs easier. They should already be doing their jobs, or else they would no longer be part of the team. Your shot, Ed."

Ed climbed into the sand trap and lined up his shot. Unfortunately it took two tries to get the ball out of the bunker and onto the green. Frustrated, he flipped his club out onto the grass and grabbed the rake, grumbling as he raked the sand smooth.

Carl, squatting by his ball, observed, "Well, Ed, I think it's still you." Two more putts and Ed's ball finally dropped to the bottom of the cup.

As he fished his ball out of the hole, Ed said, "Okay young man, let's see you make us proud." He stepped away from the hole.

Carl had been carefully considering his birdie putt. He straightened, took his stance, and lined it up. Drawing the putter head back, he sent the ball on its way. It looked like the ball was headed straight for the center of the cup, but at the last moment it veered, caught the left edge of the cup, and lipped out. The men simultaneously let out a loud groan.

"You were robbed again!" exclaimed Ed, as Carl tapped in for the easy par.

"Oh well," sighed Carl, "probably my best chance for a birdie at Pebble. But I'll take it anyhow." He laughed.

As they prepared to head to the next tee, Carl finished the previous train of thought. "Like I said before, just because you ask what your team needs, it doesn't mean you guarantee that they'll get what they request, or that you'll even agree with the request. Asking is what keeps the discussion open, and also lets you see what some of their critical issues are." Carl started walking to the next hole.

Trotting to catch up, Ed called, "With my guys, it sounds like it could be an unproductive discussion. I'll give you an example. If I ask my warehouse guy what would make his job easier, he'd probably say that we would have to rearrange the entire warehouse floor to suit his needs."

Stopping short, Carl turned and looked at Ed. "So, what would be the issue with that?"

Ed looked surprised at the question. "Do you know how much time that would take? We probably would grind to a halt during the reconfiguration!" He was almost sputtering.

Carl, picking his words carefully, answered, "Was there any chance that those suggestions would have improved the flow of the warehouse?" The golfers reached the tee area for the 8th hole.

Ed leaned on his golf bag and replied, "When we discussed it, it did sound like there was some potential, but I wasn't convinced that it would have enough payback, given the amount of time we'd be down."

"But if his suggestions really did improve the flow of your warehouse, wouldn't it be worth considering?"

Ed yanked out his driver and shot Carl a look, eyebrows knit in irritation. "What now, are you siding with my warehouse manager? I told you I didn't think there was enough payback!"

Keenly aware that Ed's emotional roller coaster was in motion again, Carl backed off. "Okay, let's play golf. Let's see … 8th hole, 416 yards. This is the one where your second shot will fly over the Pacific Ocean to get to the green."

"Go ahead and tee it up," growled Ed, still fuming at the thought of his warehouse manager.

Carl bent over and pushed his tee into the ground. Straightening up again after placing his ball on the tee, he looked out on the water, took a deep breath, and exhaled slowly.

Turning to his playing partner, Carl locked in eye contact and said, "Look Ed, I'm going to ask you one more time, then I'll leave it alone. I think I've got some business principles that you might find interesting and maybe even a little useful. But if you're going to get all worked up when we talk about it, then we should just quit talking about it. Because at the moment, it's a lot more pleasant being with Ed the golfer than being with Ed the company president."

Carl broke the gaze, turned his back, and walked over to where he stood behind his ball, lining up his tee shot. Looking down the fairway, he said, "So, which is it? Do you want to keep talking business while we play golf? Or just play golf?"

There was an uncomfortable silence for a moment. Ed studied his hands as he slowly swung his club back and forth. He looked up with a mixture of embarrassment and discomfort. "I apologize … again. It's part of the bind that I'm in. This stuff gets me so riled up, but honestly, I'm not even sure how to turn it around."

He walked over to where Carl was standing. "I definitely would like to hear more about your FORE system. I need to look at my situation differently, so I could probably stand to hear about something new." Ed laughed nervously. "And I'll try to keep my outbursts to a minimum for the rest of the round!"

"You'd better," said Carl good-naturedly. "Or else I'm going to shank one in your direction sometime." He grinned.

"Okay, lay it out there, Carl!" Ed turned and stepped out of the tee box. After his routine, Carl launched his ball, which started straight but faded slightly to the right. It landed in the short grass and rolled to the edge of the first cut of rough.

"I'll take it." Carl stooped to pick up his tee, and stood to the side as Ed approached.

Ed stopped for a moment to survey the landscape. "So, I need to be careful with my slice here, I suppose, especially on the second shot."

"Well, if you go a little right, that gives you a better angle on the green," replied Carl. "That is, unless you go too far right." He nodded at the water.

"Don't go putting those thoughts in my brain," snarled Ed. He went through his routine and hit his tee shot, which also started straight, then faded further than

Carl's did. The ball landed short of Carl's and further right, in the rough.

"That'll work," said Ed striding over to his bag.

The two men fell in step with one another. Carl turned to Ed.

"Okay, so we last left our other discussion at Aerial View #2, 'Find the right teammates and make their jobs easier.' Are you ready for Aerial View #3?"

Ed shrugged in mid-stride. "Sure, go ahead."

"I think you'll find this might even fit your second shot coming up here," said Carl. The men were approaching Ed's ball. "This is Aerial View #3:"

Aerial View #3

Let it fly. And get out of the way.

Ed looked amused as he sized up where his ball lay. "Now how would that help me with my next shot?"

"Simple. Look where your ball needs to travel to get to the green." Carl pointed to the flagstick in the distance. The ball would have to fly over the chasm created by the wall surrounding the ocean inlet.

Carl grinned at Ed. "You're going to have to trust the situation, aren't you? Line it up, pick the club, fire away, and don't worry about coming up short." He pointed at the steep walls leading to the ocean waters lapping below.

"Just like in business," continued Carl. "You pick the right team, communicate the strategy, make sure that you're lined up at the same target, and then let it fly, trusting your teammates to do their jobs."

Ed looked at Carl with one eyebrow raised. "If only it were that easy."

"I didn't say it was easy," countered Carl. "I just said that you let it fly."

"Besides, don't forget that I have a personnel problem," complained Ed. "And you do seem to have better folks to choose from where you are."

"Dammit man, will you let it go!!"

Carl's outburst made Ed recoil in surprise. He lost his grip on the club he was holding and it dropped to the ground.

"You've *got* to let go of that negative view of your people!" Carl's eyes were alive with his passion on the topic. "Maybe you could start seeing where you can leverage their strengths instead of constantly moaning about their weaknesses. Then take their weaknesses and try to compensate for them, or eliminate them."

"But it is one of the biggest issues for me," protested Ed. He had retreated a couple of steps away.

"Well," replied Carl, calmer now, "you can't fire them all, you know."

Ed nodded in silent agreement.

"Hey! Let's play some golf. It's your shot." Carl suddenly broke into a grin, causing Ed to wonder what he had just witnessed.

Still eyeing Carl warily, Ed stepped up to his ball to survey the situation. He had a straight shot at the green, but any slice would put his ball in danger of meeting the rocks or water below. He turned to Carl for feedback.

"Maybe I should aim left and if my slice kicks in, I'll still have some landing area to work with. Better than ending up on the rocks below."

Carl nodded. "Makes sense. But you still have to let it fly and trust it." He grinned again.

After one more look to line up his aiming spot, Ed stepped up to his ball. He took his stance, looked down the target line, back at the ball, and took a deep breath. With the ball on its way, he stood back to see the result. The ball started on a pull-left trajectory, then the slice took over. When the ball landed it lay safely on the fairway approach to the green, between the two bunkers.

"Woo-hoo!" Ed let out a whoop, pumping his fist. "I'll take it!"

Carl smiled broadly at Ed's jubilation. "See what happens when you 'let it fly and get out of the way'?"

"Yeah, right." Ed's skepticism was apparent as the two men strolled over to where Carl's ball lay. Carl ignored the sentiment as he surveyed his upcoming shot.

"I think I'm going to go for it," he announced. "I'm going to let it fly to the green. How often am I going to have a chance like this at Pebble Beach?"

Stepping up to his ball, Carl went through his routine and let it fly. The ball flew straight, curled to the right just a bit toward the end, and landed on the green. It rolled through and off to the left side, stopping in the first cut of fringe.

Mouth agape as he watched the ball flight, Ed said, "Wow. I think I've seen that shot on TV somewhere." He turned to Carl. "Nice golf shot, young man."

Carl laughed. "Thanks. And also for repeatedly calling me young."

As they walked to the green, Ed turned to Carl and said, "How old are you, anyhow, if you don't mind me asking?"

With a bemused grin, Carl answered, "I can't reveal all my secrets. Let's just say I concentrate on maintaining a relaxed and confident look."

"You definitely succeed at that," admitted Ed. "I'm guessing you're 20 years younger than I am."

Without addressing Ed's implied question, Carl said, "Actually, I think it has a lot to do with my being able to create some balance and get away on vacations. Believe it or not, the FORE system has allowed me to put the type of team in place where I can leave and not worry about things very much." He looked at Ed's silver, almost-white head of hair. "Maybe you ought to try it sometime."

Self-consciously, Ed ran his hand through his hair. "Based on your results, I might have to."

The golfers reached Ed's ball location. He was able to put his ball onto the green about 20 feet from the hole, below it. Carl chipped his onto the green, running it to about 5 feet below. Both men missed their par putts, but made bogey.

Walking off the green with putter in hand, Carl said, "Well, two bogeys aren't bad. This is one of the harder holes at Pebble, you know."

"And another one is right in front of us," observed Ed. "Before we tackle it, let me make sure I understand what you've been telling me. We've been talking about the "O" in FORE, "Offload", right?"

Carl nodded.

"And the two Aerial Views are #2, 'Find the right teammates then find out what makes their jobs easier,' and #3, 'Let it fly. And get out of the way.' Right again?"

"Absolutely." Carl nodded emphatically.

"Bottom line, I find the right folks, let them do their jobs, trust them, and get out of their way. I hate to bring this up again, but what if I don't have the right skill mix in the group?"

Carl pointed at Ed. "That's fair, but as I said before, you try to identify their strengths and leverage those. Take their weaknesses and either help them overcome those, or work around them. Of course, if someone is really not a match, you might have no choice but to move them out."

Carl finished wiping his putter head with his bag towel and returned the putter to its place. "You just can't fall into the trap of thinking you can't get good people anymore. You take some of the people who are not perfect fits, and make them better fits."

Ed nodded slowly as he studied his shoe tops, rubbing the side of his jaw with his right hand. "I think I'm beginning to hear you on that point." He suddenly dropped his hand and looked up. "Let's tackle the 9th. Whoever gets birdie buys the beer later!"

"Hah!" snorted Carl. "Then it won't be me." The golfers started walking to the 9th tee.

Recap – "O" is for "Offload"

In this FORE phase, "O" means **Offload**. When you focus on building the right team, you create the powerful and productive situation of being able to delegate key objectives to your teammates. They get to excel doing the things they were hired to do, and you get to excel continuing to be the leader that you should be.

We were exposed to two more Laws of Business Gravity™ that apply to this phase of the FORE system. One of them was

Second Law of Business Gravity.

"Having all the answers is not the answer to growth."

You are not the source of answers for how your teammates and associates should be doing their jobs – they are. If they occasionally need some guidance, then guide, but don't manage. Even with your guidance, let them figure out the best way, because they usually are the best equipped to do so. If you start supplying all the answers, that usually leads to micromanagement. Worst of all, you wouldn't be offloading like you should be.

To help defy the Second Law of Business Gravity, rely on the next Aerial View™:

Aerial View #2. Find the right teammates, then find out what makes their jobs easier.

The right people for your company will know what it takes for them to excel, and they will have the organization's goals in mind as well.

(Recap continued on next page…)

(... continued from the previous page)

The other Law of Business Gravity to reckon with in the "O" phase of FORE is

Third Law of Business Gravity.

"Hiring people who are too much like you, or who like you too much, will limit your growth."

To defy the Third Law, you assemble a diverse and talented group around you. If your team is too much like you, you don't get any diverse points of view, just more of your own. If you surround yourself with people who like you too much, you won't hear much bad news or anything they think you don't want to hear. They'll spend more time trying to decide what you want to hear rather than deciding on the right things to do.

As you cultivate the right mix of people in your organization, Aerial View #3 is the essence of defying both Second and Third Laws of Business Gravity:

Aerial View #3. Let it fly. And get out of the way.

Trust it. Let it fly. Let your people do what they do best. Don't hold them back with an overabundance of restrictions, guidelines, or watch-its. After you've figured out what they need to make their jobs easier, get out of their way so they can excel and make all of you look good.

Find ways to leverage your teammates' strengths. Work around their weaknesses by mitigating those or compensating for them. Don't moan about someone's lack of motivation; find out what motivates him and amplify it.

Many leaders let their organizations fly, secure in the knowledge that their vision, guidance, and motivation help their teammates reach their full potential.

Chapter 4 – "R" is for "Review"

C lubs in hand, Carl and Ed stood at the tee of the 9th hole, one of Pebble Beach's most difficult, and surveyed what lay ahead with a mixture of awe and apprehension. The fairway stretched in front of them, an undulating green carpet wrinkled and bunched up in places. Deep bunkers guarded the left side, with one choking off access to the green. Water from the Pacific lapped in from the right, and a haze lay like a translucent white blanket between the surface of the water and the distant mountains beyond.

"462 yards, par 4," announced Carl. "Bad enough that it's a long par 4, but look how little room we have to squeeze onto the green!"

"Yeah," agreed Ed. "And there's that bunker on the left guarding the entrance. Even if I tried to stay away from that, I could end up in the ocean on the right!" He shook his head and looked at Carl. "Well, you still have honors, so I think I'll wait and see what you do."

"Thanks a bunch." Carl grinned and pulled a tee out of his pocket. He bent to push tee and ball into the ground. "I think I'll try to stay on the left side for the tee shot." He let it fly. The ball rose, arced, and came down rolling just past the first set of fairway bunkers on the left.

"Nice shot," said Ed as he started to take his turn. "Now let's see if I can do the same thing." Ed's shot started left, but again his slice took over and the ball ended up near the right edge of the fairway.

As the men stowed their clubs and started walking to their balls, Ed turned to Carl and asked, "Let's get back to your FORE cycle. Is there anything else about the Offload phase that I need to know?"

"I think we've covered all of the high points on it," replied Carl. "Let's move on to the 'R' phase, for 'Review'. There's also another one of my Laws of Business Gravity that goes with this phase of the FORE cycle."

"Okay, let me guess." Ed didn't break stride, his eyes focused down the fairway. "In the Review phase, you stay on top of your team and make sure they do the right things?" He looked over at Carl for confirmation.

"Well, sort of, but not quite," answered Carl, shaking his head. "When you say 'stay on top of your team' that might imply some micromanagement, which you don't want to do." Ed bristled at the mention of the word micromanagement, but Carl pretended to not notice as he continued.

"I like to characterize it as being connected rather than being on top of things. So I focus on setting up the structures that allow me to stay connected to what's going on."

"What kind of structures do you mean?" asked Ed as the men reached the location of his ball.

Carl looked to his right out on the ocean view. "Things like staff meetings, reporting, targets, numbers as they come in … stuff like that. Man, I still can't believe this view!" He made a sweeping gesture toward the ocean, the haze blanket still visible suspended in mid-air.

"I do a lot of those things now," said Ed, a touch defensive. "When I'm in town I spend a half day each week with my guys so I know exactly what they're up to. And as you now know, when I'm not in town, I still have to call in to give guidance." He pulled an iron out of his bag to prep for his next shot.

Carl stopped in the middle of a stretching motion. "A half day each week? Isn't that a lot of time for a staff meeting?"

"We have a lot to cover." Ed took a couple of practice swings. "Why, how long are your staff meetings?"

"On average, 30 to 40 minutes each week, but no more than an hour," replied Carl. "If there's an issue big enough to need more time, we schedule a separate meeting to address it."

Ed stared in disbelief. "How can you get anything done in 30 to 40 minutes? By the time I cover what I want to, and let each person cover their agenda, we're halfway through the morning."

"Go ahead and hit." Carl gestured to Ed's ball. "I'll tell you afterwards."

Ed hit a low line drive that crossed the fairway and rolled to a stop at the left edge, in between the greenside bunker and the pair of bunkers before that. He snorted.

"Way short, but at least I have a more manageable shot to the green."

"I think you'll be fine," agreed Carl.

"So tell me the secret to a 30 minute staff meeting." The golfers started walking over to Carl's ball.

"Part of it is that we all receive 'dashboard' summaries of our key numbers in advance of the meeting. That's so we don't spend any time in the meeting going over numbers that we can read for ourselves." Carl decided on his club selection and pulled it out of the bag. He started to swing the club freely.

"The other part is that I usually don't take any of the meeting time for my agenda items, because I seldom have any. My teammates bring issues to the table and we discuss them there." Carl was eyeing his target line and getting ready to hit.

Ed waited until Carl swung. The ball lifted into the sky, its white form sharply outlined by the clear blue, and headed to the green, on line with the flagstick. As the ball descended, it looked like it was going to land in the greenside bunker, and Carl urged his ball on.

"C'mon, stay up, stay up!"

The ball hit the very top edge of the bunker, took an odd high hop, bounced twice and rolled to the back left edge of the green.

"Whew, what a shot!" gushed Ed. He clapped Carl on the shoulder. "Nice going."

"Lucky, but I'll take it anyway." Carl grinned and nodded his head. The men set off for Ed's ball.

Ed returned to the topic at hand. "You said your meetings are short because you have dashboard reports. Tell me more?"

"We have these summary reports that show us the latest key numbers that we track, things like inventory levels, turns, backlog, orders … the usual suspects. Each of my team members has key metrics that they track for their groups, and those are an integral part of how we track our progress against our goals."

Carl started drawing an imaginary figure in the air. "The report looks sort of like a dashboard instrument panel, so we can eyeball the report pretty quickly. We spend our meeting time discussing any issues in each of the functional areas." They reached Ed's ball, laying just in the first cut of rough. "Okay Ed, lay a high soft one up there and roll it in."

"Yeah, right." Ed selected a short iron, and went through his routine. His ball lifted high, on line with the flag, and came down onto the green, rolling through the back edge and into the fringe.

"All right!" Carl offered a high five, which Ed took. "Nicely done." The men started walking to the green, bags in hand.

"So you guys have key numbers that you watch? We do too, but it takes us awhile to go through them and review the results. And we can't cut back on that, either, we need to watch our numbers." Ed looked at Carl, waiting for his response.

"You shouldn't cut back on keeping tabs on your key numbers. That's the next one of my Laws of

Business Gravity that applies to this phase. Here, take a look at the card I gave you to see what it is."

Ed pulled out the card and Carl pointed to the Law he was referring to.

FOURTH LAW OF BUSINESS GRAVITY.

'YOU KNOW NOTHING IF YOU DON'T KNOW YOUR NUMBERS.'

"The numbers are important to us, but we don't get buried by them," Carl continued. "Like I said before, we don't take any meeting time reviewing the numbers. We assume that everyone has reviewed the dashboard reports before they come to the meeting. The discussion centers on any questions about why the numbers are better than expected or worse than expected." The golfers arrived at the green and dropped their bags to the ground. Taking their putters, they stepped up to the putting surface.

Ed stopped. "Wait, I'm going to get a 7-iron in case I decide to chip and run it at the hole." He backtracked to his bag while Carl headed for his ball to line up his putt.

For the next several minutes the golfers concentrated on their games. Ed chipped onto the green and rolled to within 8 feet, but took two more strokes to put the ball in the hole. Carl, laying two at the back left edge, tried a long birdie putt, bringing him to about 2 feet from the hole.

"And the crowd is hushed," said Ed in a mock whisper as if he was a golf commentator. "Will Carl be able to par the tough 9th hole at Pebble Beach?"

Carl stepped up, checked his putt line, took his stance, and rolled the putt. It clattered at the bottom of the hole.

"Yes!" He pumped his fist twice. "I love this game."

"Nicely done, young man." It was Ed's turn to offer up a high five.

Carl took a deep breath and exhaled. His face was flushed. He looked like a kid who had just gotten his most wished-for gift on Christmas. "I can't believe it. I never thought a par could be so exciting."

The men started walking to the 10th hole. "On to the last of the oceanside holes until we get to 17, huh?" said Carl, still bubbling from his triumph on the 9th.

"Yep," replied Ed. "Okay, back to business first. You guys get your reports beforehand, and spend your time in the meeting talking about why any numbers might have missed their targets."

"Or exceeded their targets, too," Carl reminded him.

"Well, not much to talk about there, just a pat on the back and a 'keep it up', right?"

"More than that, actually." Carl was again marveling at the ocean view as he spoke and walked. "If we exceed a target we take a little time seeing if there was anything we did that created that result. If so, we try to keep doing whatever it was. But we can't always take credit for success." Carl smiled and shrugged his shoulders.

"I just can't see how you can get everything done in 30 or 40 minutes each week," complained Ed.

"Like I said, everyone must review the dashboard reports before they enter the room. We don't backtrack for anyone. If someone is not prepared, they don't get to ask questions." Carl extended his arm, palm down, to emphasize his point.

"Second," he continued, "I let my team members drive the meeting, with the summary bullets on the dashboard reports setting the agenda. It really does end up being a pretty efficient discussion."

"Sounds like it." Ed nodded his head grudgingly.

"When you think about it, none of my guys want to get stuck in a long meeting anyway. They all want to get back to their work. I try to accommodate them by not keeping them too long."

The men were now standing at the 10th hole tee area, holding their drivers. Their view of the flagstick offered a combination of colors and textures. Off to the right, blue waters swept gently into the shallow sandy beach. Straight ahead, the smooth fairways and green rough were sharply outlined by the brown cliff walls that fell away to the narrow beach below.

Carl stuck his tee and ball into the ground and walked back to where Ed was standing. "Are your meetings longer because you have to review the numbers before discussing them?"

"Yes. That's because we don't get the reports until just beforehand." Ed scratched his head. "But I suppose I could ask for them earlier."

"Or hold the meeting a little later." Carl was twisting gently, preparing for his tee shot.

"Then I go through my agenda items, before I turn it over to each of them to hear what they're doing."

Carl walked back to his ball and started to take his stance. "But that shouldn't take very much time, right?"

"Depending on what's going on, it could be an hour or more."

Carl stopped in the middle of his practice swing and looked up in surprise. "An *hour* or more? What do you talk about?"

Ed sounded defensive again. "Hey, there's lots of issues I have to follow up on with my team. Things that I need to ask about in case they fall through the cracks. As I told you, sometimes there's not much initiative on display!" He was jabbing his driver in Carl's direction as he spoke.

Carl held up his hand. "Nothing intended. Just asking out of curiosity. Well, here goes with the tee shot!"

Carl's ball started to the left side of the fairway, until a bit of fade urged the ball back toward center. It landed and rolled to the right side, following the slope of the fairway.

"Humph, another nice shot," muttered Ed as he stepped up for his turn. Carl glanced at him, unsure if that was a compliment or not.

Ed went through his routine, appearing a bit edgy after the last exchange. He swung and hit the ball thin, pulling it left at first. The ball traveled low until its slice took over, pushing the flight back in line with the fairway. When it came to a stop, the ball was just inside the start of the fairway.

"That'll work," called Carl as he strode off.

Ed dumped his club back in his bag and hurried to catch up with Carl.

"All right, let's say I cut back on the length of my staff meetings," conceded Ed as he fell in step. "What else is part of this Review phase of the FORE cycle?"

Glancing out of the corner of his eye to see if Ed really meant it, Carl replied, "There are a couple of Aerial Views that go with this phase. Got your card? See for yourself, #4." He pointed to it.

Aerial View #4.

Criticize like a pro.

Ed stopped to read the small print on the card. He looked up. "Like a pro? Meaning?"

"Meaning constructive criticism, and feedback that is concise and to the point." Carl started walking again. "No long winded complaints or critiques, like a couple of bosses I've had the misfortune to work for."

"I don't give long winded critiques!" exclaimed Ed. "Besides, if someone deserves to be read the riot act, I'm the guy who has to deliver it."

The men had reached Ed's ball. By now, Carl was beginning to look upon Ed's occasional rants as mildly amusing.

"Will you let it go?" Carl was careful to say this with a smile. "I'm not talking about you, I'm just making a point here."

"Sorry," mumbled Ed.

Carl laughed. "As I was saying, criticizing like a pro involves giving genuine feedback that gets to the core of the issue. It's concise, doesn't get personal, and offers some suggestions for improvement."

Ed was scoping out his next shot. "Okay, I think I've got it. Now give me a moment to line up my next hit."

He looked down the fairway and pulled out a wood. "Looks like I can just take it straight in from here." Stepping up to his ball, he let it fly.

"Oh give me a break!" shouted Ed, slamming his club into the fairway grass. The ball started straight, but Ed's chronic slice took hold and started curving the ball in the direction of the ocean. It flew well past the edge and landed in the cascading water with a silent splash.

"Might as well hit another one here," Ed seethed. He fished another ball out of his bag and dropped it onto the fairway grass. Lining it up, he swung again.

This time the ball went pretty straight, staying in the fairway approaching the green.

"Laying 4 and I'm not even on the green yet." Ed clunked his club back in his bag and the golfers started walking over to Carl's ball.

"Hmm," said Carl lining up his sights they approached his ball from behind. "I might have a fair shot of getting to the green in regulation." He turned to Ed with a grin.

"Getting cocky, after sinking that par putt on the 9th hole, huh?" Ed shook his head. "You fearless types. I don't want to make you think too hard, but don't forget the water on the right." He flashed Carl a snarky grin.

Carl selected his club, lined up his marks and took his stance. After a practice swing, he let it fly. The ball started on line with the flagstick then started to drift to the right. It hit the ground just in front of the green, rolled through the right edge and off into the deep grass, down the slope and out of sight.

"You think you're in the water?" Ed almost sounded hopeful.

Carl shook his head. "Nope, I think it's stuck in the long grass. Should be dry, but I'm going to have to dig it out."

The golfers started their walk to the green. Ed turned and said, "All right, you've told me about Aerial View #4, 'Criticize like a pro.' Did you say there was another View that goes with this Review phase?"

"Right." Carl nodded. "Take a look at your card again, see #5?"

Ed stopped for a moment to read the card.

Aerial View #5.

"Catch good people doing great things."

He looked up with a smirk. "Well, in my place, that would be hard to ..." Ed trailed off as he caught sight of Carl's warning look. "Anyway, tell me more about it."

The men started walking again, Carl's gaze focused on some point beyond the green. "It's just that. Catch good people doing great things. Everyone is capable of doing great things. You just have to catch them at it, recognize them for it, and get them to remember it so they can do it again and again. And so others can think of other great things they can do."

They arrived at the green, and Carl headed off to the right side to look down the slope for his ball. "There it is," he said, stroking his chin. "That will be some shot. I'll be lucky that I don't end up in one of the bunkers over there." He gestured to the left side bunkers.

Ed was scratching his head again, still thinking about the latest Aerial View. "Fill me in here. What do you mean, 'catch people' doing great things? If they're doing great things, you would know it."

Carl flipped his wedge and caught it by the hosel. "I think it's human nature to focus on catching people doing something wrong. And when they do, they say

---

'Aha, I just caught you. You'd better shape up.' That's just a natural tendency, like catching our kids up to no good."

He turned and took a step to go down the slope to his ball. "So instead of watching out for when someone messes up, why not watch out for someone doing something great? Sometimes those great things aren't as obvious."

With that, Carl started down the tall grass. "Okay, here I go. Throw me a rope if I yell out!"

Ed stood there watching while Carl's head descended until it was almost out of sight. A moment later the ball came flying up from below, landing on the green and rolling to the left edge.

"Wow!" exclaimed Ed.

Carl came running up the hill, craning his neck to get a look. "How did I do?"

"See for yourself. That's a good one, all right."

"And I might even be able to save par." Carl winked. "Anyhow, you're up."

Ed lined up behind his ball and prepared to make his chip shot. Unfortunately, his club came down heavy and chunked the ball, sending it only a few feet forward to the edge of the putting surface. "Will you look at that!" he said exasperatedly, almost throwing his wedge into his bag and reaching for his putter.

"Looks like you're still away," reminded Carl gently. Ed glared at him.

Two putts later for both golfers, they were in the hole. "Bogey for you, triple for me," said Ed with a sigh. "I've got a few of those so far today."

As the men put away their clubs and prepared to head to the 11th hole, Ed's thoughts returned to the last Aerial View. "What did you mean when you said that great things are not always as obvious as bad things?"

Carl stooped to retie the laces on one of his golf shoes. "Think about it. When something bad happens, we probably know about it pretty soon, right? The phone doesn't have dial tone, the order entry system goes down, a customer cancels a big order, things like that."

Ed nodded, listening carefully.

Carl stood up. "What if someone did something that actually makes it harder for bad stuff to happen? What if he or she put something in place that kept that order entry system up, or brought in more customers with big orders? Wouldn't you think that was a great thing?"

Ed shrugged. "I suppose so. Depends, I guess."

"Depends on what?" asked Carl, palms upturned.

"Well, it depends on whether that improvement, or whatever, really made that difference. We might not know that until later, anyhow."

"*Exactly* my point," said Carl, stabbing a finger in Ed's direction. "That's what I mean when I say great things are less obvious, and that you have to watch out for them. You might not know until later how great that action was, so you would have to think back and realize that the benefit came from someone thinking ahead."

Ed thought for a moment and nodded slowly. "I see your point, and I don't necessarily disagree. But you've got to admit, when you're up to your waist fighting alligators, you don't always have a lot of time to contemplate things."

"It seems that way, but you have to find a way to turn the tide and look at things from a positive angle." Carl started to walk again, with Ed alongside.

Carl stroked his jaw and continued. "It's a different spin on the 'half full, half empty' water glass analogy. Same amount of water, but the guy who looks at it as being half full is probably trying to figure out how to fill it up and get to the next level. The guy who looks at it as being half empty is probably trying to figure out how to keep it from emptying and protect his backside. Their action plans will be different because of their perspectives."

Ed looked up at a passing seagull as they approached the 11th tee. "You're not asking me to ignore the fires and only look for silver linings are you?" he asked sarcastically.

Carl shook his head. "No, not at all. I'm just saying that sometimes you have to remember to look for the great stuff. Catch your good people doing great things, and let them know. Get them to see the glass as half full, and maybe they'll keep thinking of ways to fill it up."

"Tell you what," proposed Ed. "Let's take a break from the shop talk, and play some golf for a few holes. I have to reestablish my golfing reputation with you. So far we've covered the Focus, Offload, and Review parts of your FORE system, but when we come out and head back toward the ocean again, I want to hear about the E."

"Deal. Let's go tear up the second half!" Carl pulled out his driver and got ready to hit his tee shot.

Recap – "R" is for "Review"

The "R" phase in the FORE™ cycle is for **Review**. This takes a certain amount of balance to be effective. You want to be able to review the progress of activities to be sure that you and your team are on track, but you do not want the review process to turn into the main event.

Consider the notion of "being connected" to your teammates, instead of being "in control". Have the right level of controls, like staff meetings and reporting mechanisms, but remember that the controls are tools and not objectives.

The importance of being informed is to defy the Law of Business Gravity™ for this phase of the FORE cycle:

Fourth Law of Business Gravity.

"You know nothing if you don't know your numbers."

When you analyze how well you achieved your numbers, don't focus only on the missed targets. Try to discover the reasons why you exceeded other targets, and encourage repeating that behavior.

Two Aerial Views™ that help you in the Review phase are driven by motivating teammates in both situations of missing targets and meeting targets:

Aerial View #4. Criticize like a pro.

Aerial View #5. Catch good people doing great things.

When you criticize and troubleshoot, be constructive and concise with your remarks. Stick to professional critique on business-related issues. Teammates who want to do well will want to hear from you on how to improve.

Be on the lookout for people doing great things. Sometimes you have to look for greatness; it may not be obvious at first. Being connected will help you recognize the signs.

Chapter 5 – "E" is for "Encourage"

Carl and Ed concentrated on their golf games for the next few holes, talking about little more than the hole layout or the golf shot at hand. They hit from the 11th tee and proceeded down the fairway, walking away from the ocean as they neared the green. Numbers 12, 13, and 14 still offered sights of the spectacular coastal scenery, as did the view from the 15th tee.

The golfers now stood at the 16th tee, preparing for their next tee shots.

"Well, I've got three holes left to redeem myself with you." Ed had not had a good run.

Washing his golf ball then wiping it, Carl complained, "Hey, I didn't expect triple-bogey on Number 14. You beat me on that hole." The 572-yard 14th at Pebble is the most difficult hole on the course.

"Yeah, with a double-bogey." Ed grinned as he fished a club from his bag. "We were playing high-level golf," he finished sarcastically.

Carl stuck his ball and tee into the ground, straightened, and looked down the fairway. There were peeks of blue filtering through the trees in the distance. "I guess we return to the coastline after this hole. Let's see what I can do with this tee shot."

He went through his setup and let the ball fly. The ball started drawing slightly to the left, landing just beyond the edge of the island bunker in the middle of the fairway, rolling to a stop before it reached the downhill slope.

"Whew." Carl gestured as though he was wiping his brow. "For a moment, I thought it was going to land in the bunker."

"Nice shot," said Ed, nodding his head. "Now I don't want to go too far beyond that trap, right?"

"Right." Carl finished toweling his club. "There's a downhill slope just a bit beyond, and if you go too long you hit your second shot from the side of a hill."

Swinging his club gently, Ed stared down the fairway. After his routine was complete, he launched his ball.

"Give me a break!" he shouted, slamming his club head to the ground.

Ed's ball started on a line left of the fairway bunker, then his natural slice took over. The ball faded right, and appeared to be headed straight for the sand. As it came down, it struck the lip on the right side, somehow bounced almost straight up in the air, and landed on the grass, inches from sandy peril.

Ed let out a whoop. "All right! Out by the skin of my teeth!" He turned to Carl. "I planned it that way, you know," he said with a deadpan.

Carl grinned. "Whatever it takes." They slung their bags and started to walk.

Ed turned to Carl again. "Now that we're into our last three holes, I want to make sure I hear about the last part of your FORE cycle. The "E" is for encourage, right?"

Carl nodded and kept walking. "That's right. This is the motivation part of the cycle, to encourage your teammates to accomplish their best." They were nearing Ed's ball.

Ed stopped and started to look through his clubs. "So, we're talking about being a good cheerleader, rah-rah, sis-boom-bah, and all that stuff?" He made a selection and pulled it out of the bag.

"Not exactly." Carl smiled wryly at Ed's oversimplification. "My last Law of Business Gravity is related to this phase. Where's your card?" Ed reached into his pocket.

"There it is, the fifth Law." Carl pointed to the card.

FIFTH LAW OF BUSINESS GRAVITY.

'HOW YOU TREAT YOUR EMPLOYEES CREATES EITHER LIFT OR DRAG ON YOUR GROWTH.'

Ed looked up from the card with his eyebrows raised. "Lift or drag?"

"Yep. More after you hit your next shot."

Ed stowed the card back in his pocket and started to size up his next move. He stared at the flagstick on green. "Think I can make it to the green from here?"

Carl shook his head. "I wouldn't recommend it. You've got that bunker in front that looks like a Venus fly trap, and all sorts of tree trouble on the right. But who am I to say?" He raised his arms, palms upturned.

"And I'm not exactly leading you by a bunch of strokes." Ed picked a club from his bag. "So I'll take the advice. I'm going to lay up and get it to the edge of the fairway grass."

As close as he was to the lip of the bunker, Ed had to pick his stance carefully. When he let it fly, the ball actually went straight and stayed straight. It landed and rolled to a stop at the front edge of the fairway, just as he had intended.

"Nicely done," called Carl as he started to walk to his ball.

Ed returned his club to his bag and hurried to catch up. Carl stopped abruptly to survey his shot, almost causing Ed to run into him from behind.

"So again, 'lift or drag'?" Ed asked with arms folded.

Carl didn't take his eyes off the flagstick in the distance. "Just like for golf balls in flight, you want to create lift to keep your company aloft and growing. You can do that if you treat your associates the right way. If you don't, you create drag and the force of gravity takes over, dragging your company's growth to the ground." He decided on a club and pulled it from his bag.

Standing behind his ball, Carl lifted his club to find his line again. He took his stance, got ready, and let it rip, holding his follow-through pose as he watched the ball. The ball flew straight at the green and dropped onto the right side, sliding to the left until it was just about 6 feet from the pin.

Carl lowered his club and did a fist pump. "I love this game."

"Nice shot," agreed Ed. "Now tell me more about how you treat your associates 'the right way.' You're not going to tell me that you give them everything they want, are you?" He moved his hands in a gesture that emphasized the "everything."

Carl dropped his club into his bag and the two men started to walk again. "No, I'm not going to tell you that. It's all about being approachable and being in touch."

Carl looked over at Ed and continued. "The more your associates feel connected to you, the more you can cheat the Laws of Business Gravity. If they don't feel connected to you, gravity takes over and starts pulling you down." The golfers arrived at Ed's ball.

Ed started to check out his line. "I know being in touch is important. That's why I have weekly staff meetings. That's also why I have to make calls while I'm on a blasted vacation!" He started to sound annoyed again.

Carl glanced at Ed in amusement. "Take your next shot, and I'll continue after that."

Ed chose a club, idly swinging it as he squinted at the green. "Let's see if I can put it closer to the pin than you." He stepped up to his ball, went through his routine, and swung. The ball arced high, landed, and rolled through the green, narrowly missing Carl's ball. It came to a stop at the back edge of the green.

"I'll take it. Could have been a lot worse." Ed shrugged.

The men dropped their bags at greenside and took their putters. As they walked onto the green, light from the ocean glinted in the distance, beyond the 17th hole.

Carl squatted and started to look at his putt line. Eyes narrowed, studying the green, he said, "Back on this concept of being connected. It's about more than just having regular staff meetings. Your people need to feel connected to you, like you care about what they do."

"What do you mean?! I care about what they do!" Ed bristled at the implication.

Carl stood up and held up his hand. "Whoa, there you go again, Ed. I never said that you didn't care." He grinned.

Ed looked sheepish. "Sorry again," he muttered.

"You don't want to just be in touch. You want to be connected. People will then be comfortable telling you things, whether it's good news or bad news. Well, maybe they won't be that comfortable telling you bad news, but at least they'll tell you instead of avoiding it." Carl took a few steps to his right. "Anyhow, I think you're away, so go ahead and putt."

Ed ended up needing three putts to get his ball into the hole. Carl missed his birdie putt when it lipped out. He tapped in for a par.

"Man, you're just killing me, aren't you," complained Ed. "It's a good thing I'm not playing you for money."

"We're not?" Carl feigned surprise. "I thought we were playing for $1,000 a skin!" He laughed.

Ed shook his head. "All right, now tell me how I can get connected."

"Well, there are two Aerial Views that are part of this 'E' for 'Encourage' phase. Check out Aerial View #6 on your card." Carl pointed as Ed reached into his pocket again.

Aerial View #6.

Keep the Welcome mat out.

Ed, eyebrows raised, looked at Carl. "Let them come to me, then."

"Not just that, but go to them, too," answered Carl. "Wander around, see what folks are up to. Ask questions. Compliment them if it's appropriate."

The men were on their way to the 17th tee. Carl suddenly stopped short and pointed his finger at Ed. "One warning. When you wander around, resist the urge to criticize if you see something you don't like."

"Why's that?"

"You can deal with it at the proper time." Carl resumed walking in the direction of the 17th hole. "The wandering around is for you to listen, learn, and use the

'E' in FORE … encourage. If you start criticizing during your walk, people will start hiding when they see you coming. That makes it hard to get connected."

They reached the 17th tee and stood silently for a moment, taking in the view of the par-3 hole. The flag fluttered in the changing breeze. Beyond, lay the blue of the ocean waters with the mountains rising from the horizon. A couple of seagulls circled lazily overhead as if they were checking out the pin placement.

"I just can't believe I'm standing here at the 17th on Pebble Beach!" Carl was still gushing with boyish enthusiasm.

It was Ed's turn to be amused. "All right, young man, settle down. We still have two holes to play," he chided with a smile.

Carl teed up his ball and stepped back to survey the landscape. The breeze was blowing straight into his face.

"Ah, the trademark winds of the 17th!" Carl took a deep breath, exhaled, and laughed. Then he looked at the club he was holding. "With this wind, I'm going to have to take more club than this." He went to his bag and picked out another iron.

Carl looked over at Ed. "With the hole on the left side of the green, I'm just going to go for it."

Ed looked out at the pin. "Right over that monster trap?"

Carl nodded. "Hey, it's my next-to-last hole at Pebble Beach. Why play it safe? I just have to go for it!"

Ed shrugged. "Be my guest." He made a sweeping gesture toward the hole with his open hand.

Stepping up to his ball again, Carl went through his routine and let it fly. The ball rose high in the air and almost seemed to hang, fighting its way through the stronger breezes aloft. As it descended, it looked as if it was going to drop into the trap, but at the last moment, curled to the right and dropped on the green, rolling to the lower level away from the pin.

Carl fist-pumped. "The power of letting it fly!"

Ed grinned. "Nice shot. Lot of work left for a birdie, though." He teed up his ball and started to line it up.

Eyes fixed on the flagstick, Ed returned to the previous thought. "When I'm wandering around, you're saying that I should hold my tongue on things I don't like seeing?" He turned to Carl, swinging his club loosely side to side.

Carl met his gaze. "That's right. Walk around, listen to what's going on, and look for something to encourage. It is the Encourage phase of the cycle, you know."

Ed turned back to his ball, but Carl continued. "Most of all, when you wander around, don't give anyone the impression that you're out to fix something or even to find out what needs fixing. There's a time and place for that when needed."

Ed stepped up and started his routine, but paused in the middle of the address. He stepped back.

"How am I going to get my guys to raise the bar, if I don't give them something to work on?" He leaned on the end of his club as he gave Carl a questioning look.

Carl folded his arms and rocked back on his heels before answering. "Like I said, there is a place for that, like in formal team meetings or progress checkpoints. When you're wandering around informally, you want to concentrate on connecting with your associates. You want them to feel comfortable about approaching you. Keep the Welcome mat out, like it says in Aerial View #6."

He dropped his arms and put his hands on his hips. "Well, are you going to hit or what?"

Ed nodded and resumed his stance. He took a deep breath and exhaled. "Like you, I'm going to let it fly, too." When the ball flew, it started on line for the flagstick and stayed straight.

"C'mon, c'mon," urged Ed, eyes fixed on the flight of his ball. "Get up!"

The ball rose through the stiff breezes, approached the bunker's edge, and started to descend. It landed on the narrow fringe separating sand and green, and rolled onto the green, headed straight for the flag. At the last second it veered to the right and stopped about 12 inches from the cup.

Ed let out a whoop and leaped into the air, actually becoming airborne for a second. He landed with a thud, lost his balance, and fell to the ground.

"I can *not* believe it!" he yelled, flat on his back.

Grinning broadly, Carl approached with an open hand in the air. Ed scrambled to his feet and returned the high-five with the force of an NBA player who just made a monster dunk.

"That's a beauty," said Carl. He stood for a moment, taking in the sight of the green and the ocean beyond, then reached for his golf bag and started walking again.

Ed scampered to catch up. "Well, now that I've just hit the golf shot of my life, what's left for you to tell me about FORE and your Laws of Business Gravity?" He was still breathless from the excitement.

"Actually, there's only one more Aerial View, associated with the Fifth Law of Business Gravity." The golfers approached the green and pulled their putters out.

"That Fifth Law is the one about how I treat my employees creating lift or drag on my business, right?" Ed was admiring his ball placement as he asked.

"Right." Carl bent over and picked a leaf out of the path of his ball. "And Aerial View #7 is on your card, if you want to check it out."

Ed fished the card out of his pocket and eyed it. "I see it." He pointed at it on the card.

Aerial View #7.

**Infect others with the right moods.
Keep your germs to yourself.**

"My germs?" Ed raised his eyebrows again as he put the card back into his pocket.

"Right." Carl grinned as he squatted to line up his putt. "Let's see, I've got to get this up over the ridge and somehow get it close."

He stood over his ball. After a couple of practice swings, he sent the ball on its way. It rolled up the ridge, over, and to the hole, curling away to the right about three feet outside Ed's ball.

"My germs?" repeated Ed as Carl straightened up.

Carl grinned again. "Look, here's the scenario. You've set out the Welcome mat, and your people are getting comfortable with you around. They start to feel more connected to you." He started walking over to the golf balls laying near the pin.

"So your job now is to infect them with the right moods. Excitement. Hope. Ambition. Nobody can beat us now. Whatever. Infect them so they're revved up about what they do." Carl was eyeing his ball in relation to where Ed's was. "I think you'd better mark your ball."

Ed bent to mark and pick up his ball as Carl continued. "Now that they're revved up and rarin' to go, let them go. Let it fly. Don't put any negative attitudes on them. In other words, keep your germs to yourself."

"I don't have any negative attitudes!" protested Ed. He stopped, realizing what he had just said, as Carl looked at him with one eyebrow raised.

"Yeah, right." Carl looked like he had just tasted something strange. And then he burst out laughing.

"All right, young man." Even Ed had to smile. "Don't be a wise guy."

Ed thought for a moment. "If I promise to keep my germs to myself, will you putt out so I can finally try for a birdie?"

Carl chuckled and stepped over to his ball. His was a par putt of almost four feet, but it caught the edge and didn't drop. With a sigh, he tapped in for the bogie.

"All yours, Mr. Woods." Carl bowed to his playing partner.

Ed looked carefully at his putt, circling around the ball and the hole. He lined up the stroke for the last time, and prepared to putt. The ball rolled straight at the hole and dropped into the center with a resounding thunk.

"Can you be-*lieve* it!" Ed shouted, arms raised at the ocean. "A birdie on the 17th hole of Pebble Beach!"

Carl came up and extended a congratulatory hand, but Ed was too excited to even notice. In mock exasperation, he said, "If you're quite done celebrating, Ed, let's get on to the last hole before sundown." Carl grinned again. "Nicely done."

The two golfers reached the tee of arguably one of the most famous holes in all of golf. Carl stood for a moment, savoring the view of the sweeping curve of the fairway, ocean waves crashing against the rocks along the left, with the majestic clubhouse in the distance beyond the finishing green. When he stood in the tee box, Carl almost felt like he was on a ship's deck suspended out over the water.

"Well partner, one last hole." Ed turned to Carl. "And I actually get to finish with honors." He laughed.

Carl smiled and nodded. "You earned it. Lay it out there."

"Left of the trees, huh?" Ed straightened from placing his ball on the tee and began his routine. He swung away, the ball starting low and rising into the air. It kept rising, then started to fade slightly, eventually landing and rolling to a stop in the area at which he was aiming.

Carl had a quizzical look on his face. "Hey, your ball actually looked like it was staying aloft, even after I thought it would start coming down." He turned to Ed. "Are you defying the laws of gravity now?"

"Nope. Everyone knows that's impossible. But someone else has been teaching me how to defy the Laws of Business Gravity." Ed whipped the card out of his pocket like a magician plucking a rabbit out of a hat. "And I have proof!"

Carl laughed as he bent to tee up his ball.

"Are there any other Aerial Views to talk about before we part company?" asked Ed.

"No, we've covered them all," replied Carl as he took a couple of practice swings. "We've talked about the FORE cycle, the Five Laws of Business Gravity, and Aerial Views number 1 through 7."

He lined up his shot, stepped up, and swung away. Carl's drive on this last hole was a beauty, picture-perfect trajectory, landing in the exact spot he had played in his mind for so many years. The ball rolled in the fairway, left of the trees, well past Ed's ball. Carl lowered his club after his follow-through pose.

"And that, my friend, is sometimes what happens when you just 'let it fly.' " He grinned at Ed's expression still agape after watching the flight of Carl's ball.

"What a sandbagger," complained Ed, shaking his head in disbelief. The two golfers started their walk down the picturesque fairway.

"I'm referring to the business analogy too," continued Carl. "When you 'let it fly' within your own company, you can see great things happen. Do you think you might try it?" He glanced at the older man.

Ed was looking straight ahead, eyebrows knit in thought as he walked. "You know, I just might. But I'm going to have to take it gradually, though. Some of what you talked about is a little foreign to me right now." They slowed to a stop as they reached Ed's ball in the fairway.

Carl was looking down the fairway. "Remember to try to stay left with your next shot, so you can avoid that tree overhanging the green on your third shot." Grinning, he turned to Ed as he gestured toward the blue waters of the ocean. "Of course, you don't want to go too far left."

"I see that," replied Ed dryly. "Thanks for the heads-up. Well, let's see if I can 'let it fly' for another shot."

And he did. The ball rose straight and stayed straight, coming to a stop at the left edge of the fairway not far from the long thin bunker snaking along the rocks. Ed did a silent double-pump.

"Great shot," said Carl. "Now let's see if I can let mine fly, too." He launched his golf ball, another beautiful shot outlined against the sky as it flew through the air, landing beyond Ed's ball but nearer to the middle of the fairway.

He looked at Ed. "Looks like we're two for two! Let's hole it out and head home."

From there, each golfer reached the green in regulation. It took Ed three putts to hole out for a bogey. He picked up his ball and stood to watch Carl, who had already putted once and was studying a tricky downhill putt for par from 5 feet.

Carl looked at the line, and couldn't decide how the ball was going to roll. Seeing his indecision, Ed said with a smile, "Why don't you take your own advice, and just 'let it fly'?"

"Well, maybe 'let it roll', anyhow," replied Carl with a grin. "Okay, here goes." He let it roll. The ball went left, went right, went left again, looked like it was going to slide right, caught the right edge of the hole ... and dropped in.

"Yesss!" Carl stabbed his fist into the air.

Ed just shook his head and held out his hand. "What a way to end it, partner!"

The two men gathered their things and stood outside the pro shop for a moment. Carl looked up from filling out his scorecard. "How'd you do?"

"Well, 102, but at least I got a birdie and a par. How about you, young man?"

"87. No birdies, but 6 pars," replied Carl with a smile. "I'll take it." He extended his hand warmly.

"I had a great time playing Pebble Beach with you, Ed. Thank you for being such a good sport about listening to me."

"No, I should thank you," countered Ed. "You exposed me to your FORE system, 7 Aerial Views, and the Five Laws of Business Gravity. I'll be thinking about our talk and studying my card on the plane ride home." He waved the reference card Carl had given him.

"Well good luck, then," said Carl as the two men shook hands. "Let me know how it works out."

With that, the two golfers went their separate ways.

Recap – "E" is for "Encourage"

The "E" phase of the FORE™ cycle is where you **Encourage** your teammates and associates. This is so you can directly affect the last Law of Business Gravity™ and get the outcome that you want, to create lift instead of drag.

Fifth Law of Business Gravity.

"How you treat your employees creates either lift or drag on your growth."

Treat your teammates with trust and respect, and they create lift on the organization to keep it soaring. Do the opposite, and you'll run into drag in mid-flight, taking you down to the ground.

To affect this outcome, use the last two Aerial Views™.

Aerial View #6. Keep the Welcome mat out.

Be accessible. Better yet, wander around and take your accessibility to your team. But beware! When you walk around, resist the urge to troubleshoot, even if asked. The "R" phase of FORE is reserved for fixing and criticizing. In the "E" phase, concentrate on listening and learning from your team.

Aerial View #7. Infect others with the right moods. Keep your germs to yourself.

So maybe you're not having the best day. Don't infect your teammates with those feelings. Keep your germs to yourself. Instead, infect them with enthusiasm, hope, ambition, or the feeling that nobody can beat them now. Encourage your associates. Continue to allow them to "let it fly" and do what they do best.

If you can succeed in building a culture of trust and respect in an environment of open communication, you will make the Fifth Law of Business Gravity work to your advantage, and your company or organization keeps on soaring.

Epilogue – Six Months Later

It was a wintry afternoon. Carl was in his office sitting at his desk when his phone rang. He picked it up.

"Good afternoon, Carl Baxter speaking."

"Hello young man," said a vaguely familiar voice. "Are you shooting par at Pebble Beach yet?"

Carl's face lit up with a smile. "Well, maybe on only a few holes. Is this my playing partner, the famous Ed Hilland who birdied Number 17?"

"In the flesh," replied Ed with a laugh. After the two men exchanged updates on the state of their golf games, Ed explained why he was calling.

"I just wanted to tell you what it was like when I started using your FORE cycle along with your Aerial Views. It was slow going at first, because as I told you some of it is a bit counter-intuitive for me. And for my team, it was also a bit strange, because they weren't used to seeing this new behavior from me." He laughed. "At first they were probably wondering what I was up to."

Carl leaned back in his chair, listening intently as Ed continued.

"But as time went on, we all got more used to the concepts. Or maybe I should say that I got more used to the idea of 'letting it fly' and trusting them to do their jobs in the best way they can."

"Is it working?" asked Carl.

"It's still a work in progress," replied Ed. "But we're definitely headed in the right direction. And I wanted you to know that I probably would have never tried this approach if I hadn't gotten to know you at Pebble Beach during our round of golf last summer."

"Well, I'm glad you were open minded enough to give it a shot," said Carl, leaning forward to rest his elbows on the desk.

"As I told you then, I was in a quandary about what to try next, and your system gave me a methodology to work with. So I just wanted to say, thanks again. I keep your FORE reference card with me wherever I go."

The men exchanged well wishes and ended their call.

Carl turned and gazed out his window at the light snow falling. Then he got up to go see if he could catch his teammates doing some more great things.

The FORE Cycle Reference Card

f the	Use these seven Aerial View™ tips ...	To defy or affect the F Laws of Business Grav
	Aerial View #1. When you wish upon a star, make sure everyone knows what the star looks like.	**#1**. Without a long ranç company's growth will e decrease until it become
	Aerial View #2. Find the right teammates, then find out what makes their jobs easier.	**#2**. Having all the answ the answer to growth.
	Aerial View #3. Let it fly. And get out of the way.	**#3**. Hiring people who ¿ much like you, or who li much, will limit your grc
	Aerial View #4. Criticize like a pro. **Aerial View #5**. Catch good people doing great things.	**#4**. You know nothing i know your numbers.
	Aerial View #6. Keep the Welcome mat out. **Aerial View #7**. Infect others with the right moods. Keep your germs to yourself.	**#5**. How you treat your creates either lift or dra¢ growth.

About the Author

Gary Lim, M.A., is President of Aurarius LLC, the strategic and business management consulting firm he first founded in San Jose, California then relocated to Upstate New York. In addition to Aurarius, he founded CEO PrivateLine, and is a co-founder of HealthcareBusinessOffice LLC. His Fortune 500 experience includes executive and management positions at Hewlett Packard, ROLM/IBM, Xerox, and Novell.

An experienced public speaker, Gary has spoken to audiences in many venues. Cumulatively, his speaking engagements have been attended by well over 10,000 attendees, through keynote addresses, conference workshops, corporate/executive seminars, product launches, and training courses.

Gary's experience and skill set are focused in the areas of helping companies achieve even higher levels of performance. He utilizes his proprietary methodology to take firms to what he calls the **AgileXnt™ Zone** (pronounced a-jil-EX-ent), where organizations are both agile and excellent. In his work with client companies and seminar attendees, Gary is often considered one of the best at assessing an intricate situation, reducing it to a few key issues, and offering practical solutions.

He earned a Bachelor's degree *cum laude* from Princeton University in electrical engineering and computer science, and a Master's degree in organizational management from University of Phoenix. His first book, *The Road to Gumption: Using Your Inner Courage to Balance Your Work and Personal Life*, was an Amazon #1 Bestseller in its category.

For more information on speaking engagements, corporate seminars, or volume purchases of this book:

Book Web site:	www.LetItFlyBook.com
Company Web site:	www.AurariusLLC.com
Email contact:	info@AurariusLLC.com
Phone contact:	315-885-1532 (direct)

SPEAKING ENGAGEMENTS FOR LET IT FLY!^{SM}

Let It Fly!^{SM} speaking engagements and custom onsite seminars on the FORE™ System and Aerial Views™ are available for scheduling. Whether for one department or an entire division or company, the content can be customized to fit your industry and business situation. The timeframe can also be tailored to your needs as well, be it a one-hour keynote in a conference or a half-day working session to solve pressing business issues and problems.

The Let It Fly!^{SM} methodology lends itself well to a variety of venues, including:

- Executive retreats
- Strategic planning sessions
- Executive development programs
- Association conferences
- Supervisory and management training seminars
- Human resource management symposia
- Motivational events

All sessions are delivered personally by author and consultant Gary Lim of Aurarius LLC, and can be held at your corporate location, conference center, industry symposium, or other meeting venue. Contact Gary directly to discuss your needs.

Phone: 315-885-1532 (direct)

Email: info@AurariusLLC.com

www.ingramcontent.com/pod-product-compliance
Lightning Source LLC
Chambersburg PA
CBHW022112210326
41521CB00028B/311